Power and Willpower in the American Future

To argue against the widely proclaimed idea of American decline, as this book does, might seem a lonely task. After all, the problems are real and serious. However, if we take a longer view, much of the discourse about decline appears exaggerated, hyperbolic, and ahistorical. Why? First, because of the deep underlying strengths of the United States. These include not only size, population, demography, and resources, but also the scale and importance of its economy and financial markets, its scientific research and technology, its competitiveness, its military power, and its attractiveness to talented immigrants. Second, there is the weight of history and of American exceptionalism. Throughout its history, the United States has repeatedly faced and eventually overcome daunting challenges and crises. Contrary to a prevailing pessimism, there is nothing inevitable about American decline. Flexibility, adaptability, and the capacity for course correction provide the United States with a unique resilience that has proved invaluable in the past and will do so in the future. Ultimately, the ability to avoid serious decline is less a question of material factors than of policy, leadership, and political will.

Robert J. Lieber is Professor of Government and International Affairs at Georgetown University, where he previously served as Chair of the Government Department and Interim Chair of Psychology. He is an authority on American foreign policy and U.S. relations with the Middle East and Europe. He received his undergraduate education at the University of Wisconsin and his PhD at Harvard, and has held fellowships from the Guggenheim, Rockefeller, and Ford Foundations, the Council on Foreign Relations, and the Woodrow Wilson International Center for Scholars. He has also taught at Harvard, Oxford, and the University of California, Davis, and has been Visiting Fellow at the Atlantic Institute in Paris, the Brookings Institution in Washington, and Fudan University in Shanghai. Professor Lieber is the author of *The American Era: Power and Strategy for the 21st Century*, and is also the author or editor of another fourteen books on international relations, U.S. foreign policy, and energy security. He has been an advisor in several presidential campaigns. His articles and op-eds have appeared in leading scholarly journals, magazines, and newspapers. His media appearances have included the *PBS NewsHour* with Jim Lehrer on PBS TV, ABC's *Good Morning America*, NBC and CBS network news, *The O'Reilly Factor*, *BBC World Service*, Al Jazeera, and other radio and television programs in Europe, the Arab world, and Israel.

D1262427

Power and Willpower in the American Future

Why the United States Is Not Destined to Decline

ROBERT J. LIEBER
Georgetown University

CAMBRIDGE
UNIVERSITY PRESS

CAMBRIDGE UNIVERSITY PRESS
Cambridge, New York, Melbourne, Madrid, Cape Town,
Singapore, São Paulo, Delhi, Mexico City

Cambridge University Press
32 Avenue of the Americas, New York, NY 10013-2473, USA

www.cambridge.org
Information on this title: www.cambridge.org/9780521281270

First published 2012

Printed in the United States of America

A catalog record for this publication is available from the British Library.

Library of Congress Cataloging in Publication data

Lieber, Robert J., 1941–
Power and willpower in the American future : why the United States is not destined to
decline / Robert J. Lieber.
pages   cm
Includes bibliographical references and index.
ISBN 978-1-107-01068-0 – ISBN 978-0-521-28127-0 (pbk.)
1. United States – Economic conditions – 2009–   2. United States – Social conditions –
2009–   3. Exceptionalism – United States.   4. National characteristics, American.
I. Title.
HC106.84.L545   2012
303.4973–dc23   2011051169

ISBN 978-1-107-01068-0 Hardback
ISBN 978-0-521-28127-0 Paperback

PERMISSION ACKNOWLEDGMENT

Chapter 1 is updated and revised from Robert J. Lieber, "Staying Power and the
American Future: Problems of Primacy, Policy, and Grand Strategy," *The Journal of
Strategic Studies*, summer 2011: 1-22. Reprinted by permission of the publisher
(Taylor & Francis Ltd, http://www.informaworld.com).

Contents

v

Tables

Acknowledgments

It is a pleasure to acknowledge those who have provided comments and suggestions on points large and small, and from whose thoughts and advice I have benefited at various stages in the writing of this book. Not all of them would agree with my arguments, and some hold points of view with which I have taken issue in this work. All the same, these exchanges of ideas, whether individual or in seminars, meetings, or debates, have been cordial and constructive – something that is by no means to be taken for granted in the academic and policy worlds. I thus have a real debt of gratitude to Benjamin J. Cohen, Sally Cowal, Carl Dahlman, Edward Friedman, Eric Edelman, Dan Hopkins, Robert Jervis, Christopher Joyner, Christopher Layne, Keir Lieber, Nancy Lieber, Tim Lynch, Thomas Mahnken, Michael Mandelbaum, Joshua Mitchell, Henry Nau, Tom Nichols, Robert Paarlberg, Joshua Rovner, Yossi Shain, Zachery Selden, George Shambaugh, Leslie Vinjamuri, and Ruth Weisberg, as well as two anonymous manuscript reviewers. Special thanks to my assistants, Peter Henne, Thomas Larson, and especially Matthew Giebler. I am grateful for support from the Department of Government, College of Arts and Sciences, and from the School of Foreign Service, at Georgetown University.

I have benefited from the opportunity to present my ideas and engage in often spirited debate about them in venues at home and abroad. Among them have been Boston University, Harvard University, the University of London, National Defense University, the Naval War College, Wellesley College, Hebrew University of Jerusalem, the BESA Center at Bar Ilan University, Netherlands Defense College, The Hague Center for Strategic Studies, Norwegian Institute for Defense Studies, University of Oslo, University of Bergen, and Helsinki University.

As I have developed the argument of this book, some of the material has appeared in articles and essays that I have published elsewhere. Where I have directly drawn on those writings, I have footnoted the specific references. My early treatments of the subject and critiques of declinist arguments have appeared in *World Affairs* ("Falling Upwards: Declinism, The Box Set," Summer 2008), *International Politics* ("Persistent Primacy and the Future of the American Era," March 2009), and the *Chronicle of Higher Education* ("A Contested Analysis of America's Standing Abroad," *chronicle.com*, October 1, 2009). Chapter 1 enlarges and expands on a paper originally delivered at the 2010 Annual Meeting of the American Political Science Association, revised and later published as "Staying Power and the American Future" in the *Journal of Strategic Studies* (Summer 2011).

Research and writing for this book was supported in part by a grant from the Smith Richardson Foundation. I am grateful to Dr. Nadia Schadlow, senior program officer, and to the Foundation. Finally, it is a particular pleasure to acknowledge the advice and support of Lewis Bateman, an editor with exceptional qualities of wisdom, judgment, and experience that now are all too rare in the publishing world.

Robert J. Lieber
Washington, DC

Introduction

The idea that the United States is in a state of rapid, fundamental decline is now widely proclaimed. What started as speculation has in recent years become a chorus of voices and is now a pervasive din. Columnists, classical historians, international economists, European allies, Chinese generals, and the wider blogosphere pronounce and repeat the idea. For some, the transformation is welcomed and embraced, for others it is expressed with deep concern, but there can be little doubt that the notion is widely shared.

The description is driven by America's difficulties overseas and at home. The frustrations and costs of long wars in Afghanistan and Iraq, a continuing campaign against radical Islamist terrorism, the rise of China and of other emerging powers, and the challenges of coping with globalization and growing economic competition suggest that the United States has become overextended and is no longer capable of playing a leading role in world affairs. At home, the collapse of the real estate bubble, followed by financial crisis and a great recession, a lagging recovery, and destructive partisanship in the face of deepening problems of debt and deficit have led to gloomy assessments about America's economy, politics, and society.

The accompanying discourse is almost unrelentingly negative. Among the voices assessing American decline, British author and public intellectual Timothy Garten Ash writes of American (and European) "competitive decadence."[1] Historian Paul Kennedy sees Britain's imperial decline as foreshadowing that of America and asserts that "the long-term trajectory is roughly the same."[2] Political economist Clyde Prestowitz, a longtime critic of free trade policies, writes that "American decline becomes the new conventional wisdom."[3] Fareed Zakaria, a media commentator and public intellectual, asks: "Are America's Best Days Behind Us?"[4] And David Brooks, an unusually thoughtful and original *New York Times* columnist, warns of "unsustainable levels of debt, an inability to generate middle-class incomes, a dysfunctional political system, the steady growth of special interest sinecures and the gradual loss of national vitality."[5]

To argue, as I do in this book, against the idea of American decline might seem a lonely, if not futile, task. After all, the problems are real and serious. Nevertheless, if we take a longer view, the picture looks rather different, and much of the discourse about decline appears exaggerated, hyperbolic, and ahistorical. Why? For two broad reasons. First, because of the deep underlying strengths of the United States. These include not only size, population, demography, and resources, but also the scale and importance of its economy and financial markets, its scientific research and technology, its competitiveness, military power, and absorptive capacity, and its unique attractiveness to talented immigrants. Second, there is the weight of history and of American exceptionalism, or what social scientists like to call path dependency. Throughout its history, the United States has repeatedly faced and eventually overcome daunting challenges and crises, many of which gave rise to weighty and dire predictions. The most dangerous of these experiences have included the Civil War, repeated financial crises during the nineteenth century, the Great Depression of the 1930s, and

[1] Timothy Garton Ash, "Debt Crisis: In Our Competitive Decadence, We Face Eurogeddon and Dollargeddon," *The Guardian* (London), July 20, 2011, http://www .guardian.co.uk/commentisfree/2011/jul/20/us-debt-crisis-european-default, accessed July 21, 2011.
[2] Paul Kennedy, "Back to Normalcy," *The New Republic*, December 21, 2010.
[3] Clyde Prestowitz, "New wind blowing: American decline becomes the new conventional wisdom," *foreignpolicy.com*, June 15, 2011, http://prestowitz.foreignpolicy .com/posts/2011/06/15/new_wind_blowing_american_decline_becomes_the_new_ conventional_wisdom, accessed July 23, 2011.
[4] Fareed Zakaria, *TIME*, March 5, 2011.
[5] David Brooks, "Pundit Under Protest," *The New York Times*, June 14, 2011.

the geopolitical and ideological threats posed by Nazi Germany, Imperial Japan, and the Soviet Union.

However, isn't the present predicament different, especially in its foreign challenges and underlying economic dimensions, and haven't we delayed too long in responding to it?

In this book I take into account these and other factors such as the scale of globalization, foreign competition, especially from China, and the rising costs of entitlement programs. Nonetheless, in contrasting a recent past of unique American dominance and international primacy with a contemporary era of decline at home and abroad, I argue that pessimists have exaggerated the scale of both past prominence and current peril. As evidence of this tendency toward hyperbole and the volatility of received opinion, note that from the early 1990s through 2004, and in the aftermath of initial American victories in Afghanistan and Iraq, descriptions of unique American dominance and "hyperpower" were ubiquitous. Some of this treatment was admiring, some critical, but almost all of it took U.S. primacy for granted and saw it as long lasting. Nevertheless, within just a few years, the narrative had altered radically. Now America was seen in deep trouble, on both foreign and domestic fronts. Accompanying this shift in conventional wisdom, China is increasingly depicted – often in awed and uncritical terms – as the next great world power.

It is true that the United States has been slow to respond, as it often is, but here too some perspective on the past is useful. Winston Churchill famously remarked that "Americans can always be counted on to do the right thing . . . after they have exhausted all other possibilities." However, the idea can be traced back to Alexis de Tocqueville, commenting in his 1830s work, *Democracy in America*, that the virtue of Americans lay not in being more enlightened than others, "but in being able to repair the faults they commit." These observations point to a fundamental characteristic of the United States – its unique flexibility and adaptability. And it is this capacity that provides a basis for optimism in assessing America's future. The ability to change and innovate, especially in response to crisis, is unusual for a large country and especially for a great power. In short, history and past experience matter.

To be sure, there can be no certainty about America's ability to overcome current problems, and contingency and human agency come into play. Ultimately, elite and popular beliefs, policy choices, and leadership remain critical in shaping outcomes. In this sense, the challenges facing the United States are at least as much ideational as they are material. Here, however, there may be a paradox working in America's favor. It is that the worse the crisis, the greater the sense of urgency and the more likely that policy makers, regardless of their prior inhibitions and beliefs, will find themselves having to respond effectively.

The stakes are immense, and not only for America itself. Since World War II, the United States has been the world's principal provider of collective goods. The leading international institutions of today and much of the existing international order have been a product of American leadership. Evidence from recent decades suggests that the alternative is not that some other institution or major power (the UN, the EU, China, India, Russia, or Japan) will take its place, but that none will. Some have argued that the effects of globalization are leading the world toward greater cooperation and even collective security. This may be a comforting view about the implications or even desirability of American disengagement, but practical experience suggests otherwise. In dealing with failed states, ethnic cleansing, human rights, the environment, trade liberalization, regional conflict, and nuclear proliferation, emerging powers such as the BRICS (Brazil, Russia, India, China, and South Africa) have been largely unhelpful, and others in Europe, Asia, Africa, or Latin America have more often than not lacked the will or capacity to act collectively on common tasks.

For the United States, as I argue here, the maintenance of its leading role matters greatly. The alternative would not only be a more disorderly and dangerous world in which its own economic and national security would be adversely affected, but also regional conflicts and the spread of nuclear weapons would be more likely. In addition, allies and those sharing common values, especially liberal democracy and the market economy, would increasingly be at risk. Ultimately, America's ability to avoid serious decline and the significant international retrenchment that would be a result of severely reduced resources becomes a matter of policy and political will. There is nothing inevitable about decline, and both past experience and national attributes matter greatly. Flexibility, adaptability, and the capacity for course correction provide the United States with a resilience that has proved invaluable in the past and is likely to do so in the future.

In the chapters that follow, I develop these arguments and set out the case for a more optimistic understanding of the American future. Chapter 1, "The American Future: Problems of Primacy, Policy, and Purpose," begins by examining the experience of American primacy as well as the ways in which the country has responded to severe crises and external threats. In understanding these experiences, it is crucial to appreciate the importance of policy choices and leadership. It is also essential to weigh the effects of contemporary factors including the revolution in information technology, socialization and education of younger elites, and whether a sense of shared national identity has been declining. Although there has been modest erosion in America's overall capabilities, it retains the power and capacity to play a leading world role, hence the ultimate questions about its future are likely to be those of policy and will.

Chapter 2, "Domestic and Global Interactions: Economics, Energy, and American Power," assesses the impact of economic, financial, and energy issues. Additional perspective about the past is especially useful here, for example in appreciating that during the nineteenth century, the United States experienced and overcame at least five major financial crises. We also tend to forget the gravity of the depression in the 1930s as well as the severity of the recession that took place in the late 1970s and early 1980s. This too triggered gloomy assessments about the American future, and as recently as the late 1980s, it was feared that America was losing ground to a ruthless and formidable Asian competitor, Japan. However, even as dire forecasts were being voiced, that challenge was beginning to ebb. Regardless of its contemporary difficulties and serious problems of debt and deficit, America's fundamental economic strength, human resources, and science and technology remain unique and should not be underestimated.

Chapter 3, "American Attitudes and Institutions," delves into the attitudes, policies, and institutions that have shaped America's world role and determine its ability to lead. Here, public attitudes, domestic doctrines, and the unique characteristics of American exceptionalism as well as the openness of its society come into play. While a wide range of outcomes is foreseeable in the coming years, we should be skeptical about pessimistic predictions concerning the American future.

Chapter 4, "Threats to Persistent Primacy and the Rise of Others," turns from domestic affairs to the international context, in order to assess the impact of foreign threats and the rise of emerging powers. Long-term projections have been unreliable, and the past half-century has seen as many as five waves of declinist predictions. Shifts in the international distribution of power are occurring, and threats from nuclear proliferation and radical Islamist terrorism need to be taken into account. Nonetheless, the long-term record of the United States remains one of remarkable resilience, adaptation, and crisis response. The rise of China presents a unique challenge, and over the long term it could emerge as a great power competitor. However, much of the treatment of China's rise is uncritical and has overlooked or downplayed an array of internal problems that are likely to affect it. In addition, although collaboration with other countries and institutions can be helpful and even essential in responding to actual or potential threats, there is no true substitute for American engagement and leadership.

Chapter 5, "Stretch or 'Imperial Overstretch'?" asks whether America is overstretched, a question central to the entire decline debate. The question is reasonable, in view of the human and material costs of two wars as well as likely resource constraints stemming from problems of debt and deficit. Overall, the burdens of America's world role are substantial, but do not in themselves constitute overstretch. The underlying question is whether American policy elites and the public will continue to support these commitments or decide instead to embark on a course of retrenchment. In this area, too, the ability of America to sustain its international role is less a question of material limits than of judgment and will.

Chapter 6, "Power and Willpower in the American Future," begins with the question of whether the problems facing America at home and abroad really are different from those it has transcended in the past. I conclude that the difficulties are not intractable. America retains its edge, and its advantages include both material and nonmaterial elements. Much remains to be done in domestic as well as foreign policy, but the robustness of American society, coupled with its unique capacities for adaptation and adjustment, is likely once again to prove decisive.

I

The American Future

Problems of Primacy, Policy, and Purpose

"[T]he United States cannot afford another decline like that which has
characterized the past decade and a half.... [O]nly self-delusion can
keep us from admitting our decline to ourselves."

– Henry A. Kissinger, 1961[1]

In these words, one of America's most distinguished strategic thinkers
and policy makers expresses alarm at America's condition and the perils it faces.[2] The warning seems timely, yet it was written more than
half a century ago as an assessment of the Soviet threat, problems with
allies and the developing world, and in frustration with what the author
saw as dangerously inadequate policy and strategic choices. Henry
Kissinger was by no means alone. He cited George Kennan's lament
about our domestic failings with race, the cities, the education and
environment of our young people, and the gap between expert knowledge and popular understanding, even while criticizing Kennan's focus
on those problems to the exclusion of military and diplomatic threats.[3]

---

[1] Henry A. Kissinger, *The Necessity for Choice: Prospects of American Foreign Policy*
(New York: Harper, 1961), pp. 1–2.
[2] An earlier version of this chapter appeared in *The Journal of Strategic Studies*, Summer
2011. The arguments here are foreshadowed in a paper presented at the Annual
Meeting of the American Political Science Association, Washington, DC, September
4, 2010, and in my article, "Persistent Primacy and the Future of the American Era,"
International Politics (London), Vol. 46, No. 2/3 (March 2009): 119–139.
[3] George F. Kennan, *Russia, the Atom and the West* (New York: Harper, 1958), p. 13,
cited in Kissinger, p. 9.

Since World War II, the United States has been the preeminent actor in world affairs. Its status at the end of that conflict, its role in creating postwar international institutions, its leadership in the reconstruction of Europe and Japan, and its dominant status within the Western alliance during the Cold War are well known and beyond dispute. With the collapse of the Soviet Union in 1991, America emerged as the lone superpower. Yet some two decades later, its position of both absolute and relative power appears to have deteriorated. Many scholars and strategists point to economic, structural, political, and even military vulnerabilities, and contend that the United States is in serious decline. Meanwhile, the rise of important regional actors, especially Brazil, Russia, India, China and South Africa (the BRICSs), as well as others such as Indonesia, Turkey, Iran, and the increasingly prosperous and dynamic countries of East and Southeast Asia, is said to be seriously diminishing U.S. primacy in world affairs.

These depictions are pervasive on the Internet and in the press. A quick Google search for the term "American decline" yields 117 million "hits" in 0.13 seconds.[4] A columnist for *The New York Times* writes that, "Wherever you choose to look... you'll see a country in sad shape."[5] A leading German news magazine headlines, "A Superpower in Decline."[6] And from the realm of pop culture, the comic book action hero Superman renounces his U.S. citizenship.[7]

But are such assessments accurate? In a previous book, I argued that the threat from militant Islamism and terrorism, the weakness of international institutions in confronting the most urgent and deadly problems and in sustaining international order, and the absence of effective alternatives made an American grand strategy of superpower engagement a logical adaptation to the realities of the post-9/11 world.[8] The ability of the United States to maintain its position in global affairs is thus a question of immense importance, not only in terms of national

---

[4] Accessed November 22, 2011.

[5] Bob Herbert, "Hiding From Reality," *The New York Times*, November 20, 2010.

[6] "A Superpower in Decline: Is the American Dream Over?" *Der Spiegel*, November 1, 2010.

[7] Laura Hudson, "Superman Renounces U.S. Citizenship in 'Action Comics' #900," *Comics Alliance.com*, April 27, 2011, http://www.comicsalliance.com/2011/04/27/superman-renounces-us-citizenship/#ixzz1Q8JyCMZK, accessed June 23, 2011.

[8] Robert J. Lieber, *The American Era: Power and Strategy for the 21st Century* (New York: Cambridge University Press, 2007).

interest, but because the world depends on the United States as its principal provider of public goods.[9]

Central to this question is an understanding of the internal foundations on which American capability ultimately rests. As noted by British strategist Michael Howard a generation ago, these "forgotten dimensions of strategy" include not only the ability to deploy and support the largest and best-equipped military forces, but especially the capacity to preserve the social cohesion without which national power and strategy cannot be sustained.[10] In recent years, most of the analysis and debate about the American future has focused on material factors: economics, technology, human resources, or the rise of peer competitors abroad. However, to the extent that limits to American primacy do exist, they are less likely to be material than ideational in nature, in the sense of elite and popular beliefs, social cohesion, policy choices, and leadership.

Primacy Past and Present

Two propositions are widely asserted by those who see the ebbing of American predominance: first, that America itself as a society, an economy, and a political power is in decline; and second, that its international primacy is eroding as a result of the rise of other countries.

On the domestic front, the effects of a severe financial and economic crisis, an unprecedented national debt and deficit, a yawning balance of trade and payments deficits, and an aging and overloaded infrastructure lead a prominent financial journalist to foresee "the beginning of the end not just of an illusory 'unipolar moment' for the US, but of western supremacy in general and of Anglo-American power, in particular."[11] Fareed Zakaria, a widely quoted public intellectual, warns that America has become an "enfeebled" superpower and embellishes his case by observing that the world's tallest Ferris wheel is now in

---

[9] For a compelling statement of this point, see Michael Mandelbaum, *The Case for Goliath: How America Acts as the World's Government in the Twenty-First Century* (New York: PublicAffairs, 2006).

[10] Michael Howard, "The Forgotten Dimensions of Strategy," *Foreign Affairs* (Summer 1979): 977.

[11] Martin Wolf, "How the Noughties Were a Hinge of History," *Financial Times*, December 23, 2009.

Singapore and the largest casino is in Macao.[12] For good measure he adds: "America's success has made it sclerotic."[13]

As for the international arena, many scholars and pundits maintain that serious balancing has already begun. The historian Paul Kennedy, after a hiatus in which he seemed to have set aside his earlier declinist admonitions, has returned to his original theme. Writing at the height of the financial crisis in an article he titled "American Power Is on the Wane," he insisted that, "[W]hile today's Russia, China, Latin America, Japan and the Middle East may be suffering setbacks, the biggest loser is understood to be Uncle Sam."[14] More recently, Kennedy has added that "the United States is slowly and naturally losing its abnormal status in the international system and returning to being one of the most prominent players in the small club of great powers."[15] A widely cited National Intelligence Council Report, *Global Trends 2025*, foresees domestic constraints and the rise of foreign powers leading to a global, multipolar world.[16] A former president of the Council on Foreign Relations asserts, "The United States is declining as a nation and a world power."[17] These pundits and others argue that the rise of China, India, and other regional powers, the recovery of Putin's Russia, and (prior to the Eurozone crisis) the development of the European Union signal a profound shift in global power.[18]

What is striking about these conclusions is that until relatively recently, the more commonplace observations concerned America's extraordinary primacy. Consider the description by Paul Kennedy in

---

[12] Fareed Zakaria, "The Rise of the Rest," *Newsweek*, May 3, 2008; *The Post American World* (New York: Norton, 2008), pp. 48, 217; and "Enfeebled Superpower: How America Lost Its Grip," *The Sunday Times* (London), June 22, 2008.

[13] Fareed Zakaria, "Are America's Best Days Behind Us?" *TIME*, March 3, 2011.

[14] Paul Kennedy, "American Power is on the Wane," *The Wall Street Journal*, January 14, 2009, p. A13. Also see Francis Fukuyama, "The Fall of America, Inc.," *Newsweek*, October 13, 2008.

[15] Paul Kennedy, "Back to Normalcy," *The New Republic*, December 21, 2010.

[16] *National Intelligence Council*, Global Trends 2025: A Transformed World (Washington, DC: U.S. Government Printing Office, November 2008).

[17] Leslie H. Gelb, "Necessity, Choice, and Common Sense," *Foreign Affairs* (May/June 2009): 56.

[18] For example, see Christopher Layne, "The Unipolar Illusion Revisited," *International Security*, Vol. 31, No. 2 (Fall 2006): 7–41; T. V. Paul, "Soft Balancing in the Age of U.S. Primacy," *International Security*, Vol. 30, No. 1 (Summer 2005): 46–71; Robert Pape, "Soft Balancing against the United States," loc. cit.: 7–45; Stephen M. Walt, *Taming American Power* (New York: Norton, 2005).

a February 2002 *Financial Times* op-ed, contrasting America's predominance with that of other empires over the past 2,000 years:
"Nothing has ever existed like this disparity of power; nothing...
Charlemagne's empire was merely Western European in its reach. The
Roman Empire stretched farther afield, but there was another great
empire in Persia, and a larger one in China. There is therefore no
comparison."[19] Another tribute to American power in the middle of
the last decade came from the veteran Egyptian ambassador to the
United States, Nabil Fahmy, who in 2005 observed, "I cannot succeed
in pursuing my domestic objectives, economic or political; I cannot
succeed in pursuing my regional objectives... and I cannot succeed in
pursuing my global objectives... be it on social issues, on arms control
issues, on economic issues – without engaging America."[20]

Other observers were more resentful but no less impressed with
American power. For example, in the late 1990s, French foreign minister Hubert Vedrine uttered a widely quoted complaint. He defined
the United States as a "hyperpower," one that is "dominant or predominant in all categories," adding that this unique strength extended
beyond military power, economics, or technology, to encompass "this
domination of attitudes, concepts, language and modes of life."[21]

However, if the United States possessed anything even close to such
unprecedented power across so many dimensions and a degree of dominance beyond anything the world had seen in two millennia, is it
plausible that such a reversal could take place in little more than half
a decade? To be sure, two difficult wars, a severe financial crisis, and
the rise of China have made a substantial impact, but whether these
are sufficient to cause the kind of sudden tectonic shift implied in so
much contemporary discourse is far from certain.

Important events and shifts in geopolitics affect presidents and their
administrations, and changes within the United States can reverber-
ate abroad. In this context, the onset of the Obama administration
was initially acclaimed in many parts of the world. Foreign opinion
polls at first showed largely favorable views of the American president

---

[19] Paul Kennedy, "The Eagle Has Landed," *Financial Times*, February 1, 2002.
[20] Quoted in Neil MacFarquhar, "Can't Live With; Can't Live Without," *The New York Times*, January 16, 2005.
[21] Quoted in, "To Paris, U.S. Looks Like a 'Hyperpower'" *The New York Times*, February 5, 1999.

and, in many countries, improvement in attitudes toward the United States itself. The change was especially pronounced in Europe, where surveys in twenty-two countries conducted by the Pew Research Center's Global Attitudes Project found the U.S. favorability rating in Germany climbing from 31 percent in 2008 to 63 percent in 2010, and in France from 42 percent to 73 percent.[22] Results in Asia and Latin America were also positive. Although Barack Obama's ambitious outreach to Arab and Muslim populations gained him some personal approval there in the 2009 surveys, by the spring of 2010, the Pew polls showed his personal support eroding in every Middle Eastern Muslim country in which a poll was taken. Moreover, despite Obama's initiatives, these populations exhibited highly negative views toward America itself, with only 21 percent in Jordan and just 17 percent in Egypt, Turkey, and Pakistan expressing positive views.[23] A year later, and despite continued efforts at outreach and a belated but welcoming response to the Arab Spring, responses in Jordan, Turkey, and Pakistan had become still more negative.[24]

Daunting foreign policy challenges continued to confront the president and his administration, in particular a costly and difficult counterinsurgency in Afghanistan and remaining commitments in Iraq, which stretched military resources. The leaders of Iran and North Korea vilified America and frustrated U.S. policies aimed at halting their nuclear programs. Brazil and Turkey – the latter a longtime member of NATO but increasingly an ally in name only – embraced the Iranian president Mahmoud Ahmadinejad and broke ranks over

---

[22] Pew Global Attitudes Project, *Obama More Popular Abroad Than at Home, Global Image of U.S. Continues to Benefit*, June 17, 2010, http://pewglobal.org/files/pdf/Pew-Global-Attitudes-Spring-2010-Report.pdf; and "Confidence in Obama Lifts U.S. Image Around the World," released July 23, 2009, http://pewglobal.org/reports/display.php?ReportID=264. Also see *Transatlantic Trends, Key Findings 2009*, German Marshall Fund of the U.S., June 2009, http://www.transatlantictrends.org/trends.

[23] Results from the 2010 Pew Research Center poll, "U.S. Favorability Rating," question Q7a; also Q34a, "Muslim Views of Obama." Interviews conducted April 7–May 8, 2010.

[24] In the Spring 2011 Pew poll, the U.S. favorability rating in Jordan had fallen to 13%, Turkey 10%, and Pakistan 12%. Only in Egypt was there a slight improvement, to 20%. See Pew Global Attitudes Project, *China Seen Overtaking U.S. as Global Superpower*, July 13, 2011, http://pewglobal.org/2011/07/13/china-seen-overtaking-us-as-global-superpower/, accessed July 25, 2011.

Iran sanctions. Overemphasis on seeking a breakthrough in Israeli-Palestinian negotiations and an earnest but misplaced assumption about the importance of linkage (the belief that this issue held the key to virtually every other crisis in the region) proved counterproductive and retarded rather than advanced the peace process. Russia and China asserted themselves regionally and in the UN Security Council. In addition, the difficulties of crafting a new international financial architecture capable of coping with the realities of a truly global economy have prevented the reshaping of existing institutions or the creation of new ones.

Responses to Decline

Without a doubt, the United States now confronts serious problems at home and abroad. Nonetheless, recent declinist arguments carry an unmistakable echo of the past. Antecedents of these views were apparent in the 1970s, 1980s, and 1990s, and on occasion were even phrased in identical language.[25] Indeed, declinist proclamations have appeared on and off since the late eighteenth century. For example, writing in 1797, the French ultraconservative Joseph de Maistre derided the young American republic, emphasizing its "symptoms of weakness and decay."[26] A late-eighteenth-century French scientist, the prominent and widely read George Louis Buffon, even made a natural science argument for the inferiority of the New World – including its plants, animals, and people. Even though Buffon had never traveled to America, he insisted that its dogs failed to bark, its birds did not sing, and by implication its people were feebler and less intelligent. At the time, Thomas Jefferson was so infuriated by this argument that he devoted a chapter in his *Notes on the State of Virginia* to refuting it.[27]

Not only have past depictions of America warned of weakness and decline; previous crises in American history have included perils more

---

[25] For example, in 1970, a book by Andrew Hacker announced *The End of the American Era* (New York: Atheneum, 1970). A generation later Charles Kupchan borrowed the same book title to deliver his own warning in *The End of the American Era* (New York: Knopf, 2002).

[26] Philippe Roger, *The American Enemy: The History of French Anti-Americanism* (Chicago: University of Chicago Press, 2005), p. 46.

[27] Ibid., pp. 7–14.

threatening than those of today. Consider, for example, the menace
of fascism in the 1930s and then the onset of World War II against
Nazi Germany and Imperial Japan, swiftly followed by the Soviet
domination of Eastern Europe, the early Cold War years, the triumph
of Mao's communist forces in the Chinese civil war, and the outbreak
of the Korean War. In turn, there were the upheavals of the 1970s,
including a major oil shock, the loss of Vietnam, a revolution in Iran,
the 444-day American embassy hostage crisis, a second oil shock, and
then the 1979–1982 recession with record postwar unemployment,
13 percent inflation, and 18 percent interest rates.

It is also useful to recall previous conventional wisdom about rising
hegemons said to be challenging American predominance. During the
late 1970s, the Soviet Union appeared to be a daunting competitor.
Two decades ago, Japan was widely seen as on track to become the
world's dominant economic power and potential geopolitical leader.
Ezra Vogel's book *Japan as Number One*[28] not only became a best
seller; it also epitomized a then increasingly common view of what the
future held in store. As recently as a decade ago, a rapidly expanding
European Union was depicted not only as a model for the future,
but as an emerging superpower that in population, economic weight,
and geopolitical impact was not only attaining a size and importance
comparable to that of the United States, but might well become a
serious rival to it. From the vantage point of the second decade of the
twenty-first century, the paeans to Japan and Europe now seem quaint,
as both struggle with formidable economic and political problems and
neither possesses the rising-power traits so recently attributed to them.
China today is a different story and, unlike Japan and the EU, has
the potential to become a true peer competitor and superpower rival.
Previous cases, however, suggest we should be careful about assuming
this is destined to occur.

For the United States, historical as well as relatively recent comparisons provide evidence for its robustness and adaptability as a
society and as a leading power. Time and again, America has faced
daunting challenges and made mistakes, yet it has possessed the inven-
tiveness and societal flexibility to adjust and respond successfully. In

---

[28] Ezra Vogel, *Japan as Number One: Lessons for America* (Cambridge, MA: Harvard
University Press, 1979).

this regard, neither the rise of the BRICS and other regional powers, nor competition in a globalized world economy, nor "imperial
overstretch," nor domestic weakness are by themselves bound to have
the transformative effects that have been so often suggested. Despite
major changes and severe challenges, these domestic and international
constraints do not in themselves predetermine the end of America's
international predominance. All the same, just because America has
previously overcome adversity and retained both its strength and international primacy does not guarantee that it will do so now.

The impact of financial constraints, especially the current and projected burdens of debt and deficits, needs to be taken very seriously.
Michael Mandelbaum has made a compelling argument that these
conditions will require a strategy of retrenchment. He focuses on the
tenacious budgetary dilemmas that policy makers will be forced to
deal with in the coming years and that, in his judgment, will dictate a
less expansive foreign policy. Mandelbaum cites the combined effects
of expanding deficits during the previous decade, the enormous costs
of the financial crisis, and the growing burden of entitlement programs as the Baby Boom generation retires, and observes that "the
serious money . . . is to be found in the defense budget." He avoids the
facile arguments of the declinists and sees these changes as occurring
gradually and reluctantly, but nonetheless unavoidably because of the
daunting political obstacles to cutting spending on entitlement programs or increasing taxes in sufficient amounts to cope with long-term
trends in budget deficits and the national debt.[29]

Mandelbaum's argument cannot by any means be discounted, not
least because of the increasing proportion of entitlement programs in
the federal budget. Here, however, my own approach draws on two
broader considerations. First, long-term economic forecasts are often
unreliable. Even slight changes in relevant parameters produce widely
varying results the farther into the future the projections are made.

---

[29] Michael Mandelbaum, *The Frugal Superpower: America's Global Leadership in a Cash-Strapped Era* (New York: PublicAffairs, 2010); "Overpowered: Questioning the Wisdom of American Restraint," *Foreign Affairs*, Vol. 89, No. 3 (May/June 2010): 114–119; and "America's Coming Retrenchment: How Budget Cuts Will Limit the United States' Global Role," *ForeignAffairs.com*, August 9, 2011, http://www.foreignaffairs.com/articles/68024/michael-mandelbaum/americas-coming-retrenchment, accessed August 18, 2011.

Illustratively, medium- and long-term estimates of federal budget balances during recent decades have often been wide of the mark because even modest annual variances in productivity, GDP growth, employment, inflation, and tax revenues can quickly cause forecasts to become outdated. For example, even incremental improvements in economic growth rates can have a major impact over the course of half a decade. In this light, forecasts that extend to the years 2040–2050, as in the *Global Trends 2025* report, become deeply problematic.[30]

A second reason to question whether deficit and entitlement costs may compel severe cutbacks in defense and foreign policy concerns the likelihood of external threats that can motivate policy makers to maintain foreign commitments even when their preferences might have led them in the opposite direction. As a telling example, consider President Obama's ownership of two wars: Iraq, where he found it necessary to follow a pace of withdrawal notably slower than what he had advocated as a senator and presidential candidate; and Afghanistan, which he had previously identified as a necessary war, but to which, within his first year, he had to temporarily commit 33,000 additional troops, funding to support the effort, and substantial economic and military assistance to neighboring Pakistan. Moreover, as the subsequent Libyan intervention suggested, no matter how reluctant a president may be, circumstances can compel action and involvement.

In making sense of these issues, especially responses to crises, it is crucial to appreciate the importance of policy choices and leadership. Economic size, population, technology, geography, and history are some of the key variables that shape national strategies, but the element of contingency should not be underestimated. Although the material aspects of national power are of fundamental importance, they shape outcomes only in the very broadest terms, whereas specific choices by decision makers about policy become crucial.[31]

---

[30] See growth projections for 2040–2050 in National Intelligence Council, *Global Trends 2025* (Washington, DC: U.S. Government Printing Office, November 2008), pp. vi, 7, 21.

[31] Aaron Friedberg and Azar Gat have both written with considerable insight on this subject. Friedberg elaborates on the relationship between power and policy in "Same Old Story: What the Declinists (and Triumphalists) Miss," *American Interest* (November 2009): 24–34. Azar Gat has emphasized the contingency of outcomes and of America's pivotal role in defeating the two great totalitarian challenges of the twentieth century, in "The Return of Authoritarian Great Powers," *Foreign Affairs*, Vol. 86, No. 4 (July/August 2007): 59–69.

During the past two centuries, profound threats to the United States have provided the stimulus to major shifts in grand strategy. The British assault on Washington in August 1814, the Japanese attack on Pearl Harbor in December 1941, and the 9/11 attacks on the World Trade Center and the Pentagon are cases in point.[32] Other examples of threats as a spur to transformations in strategy and policy include the three twentieth-century occasions in which a hostile great power threatened to gain control of the Eurasian landmass and thereby imperil America's security and vital interests. These cases included Imperial Germany in 1917, Nazi Germany in 1941, and the Soviet Union in 1947, and they precipitated President Wilson's intervention in World War I, FDR's priority for the European theater in World War II, and Truman's commitment to containment, the Marshall Plan, and NATO in 1947–1949.

Information, Socialization, and National Identity

In each of the above cases, strategy was a product both of external threat and specific, fateful policy choices by a president and his administration, with the support of Congress. But threats are often ambiguous, and there are societal, political, and institutional reasons why creating and implementing a coherent national strategy and thus maintaining an engaged and leading international role may have become more difficult since the end of the Cold War. Three contemporary elements seem especially relevant: the revolution in information technology, problems in the socialization and education of younger elites, and erosion of the bases on which a sense of national community and solidarity ultimately rests.[33]

First, information technology and the new media intensify an environment in which the immediate drives out the important. The 24/7 news cycle, the Internet, social media, cable TV, and multiple forms of hi-tech communication in which news in its most unmediated and undifferentiated forms becomes instantly available affect everyone. On the positive side, these connect people to a wealth of information and

32 John Lewis Gaddis makes this point in *Surprise, Security and the American Experience* (Cambridge, MA: Harvard University Press, 2004).

33 On grand strategy and the need for broad education, knowledge, and vision, see Charles Hill, *Grand Strategies: Literature, Statecraft, and World Order* (New Haven, CT: Yale University Press, 2010).

to each other in unprecedented fashion. As the example of the Arab Spring vividly demonstrated, in repressive societies, the new media make it far harder for regimes to control and manipulate information.

However, these multiple inputs also expose the general public to graphic images devoid of context and without the mediation common to traditional print media or the older network news telecasts. Imagine the impact on the willingness of the American public and its elected leaders to sustain a long and bloody war if instant images of slaughtered troops on the beaches of Normandy or vivid pictures of mass civilian casualties from British and American strategic bombing in Europe had been available. In turn, for political elites and policy makers, the unrelenting flood of e-mails, memos, press inquiries, and a rapid-response news cycle increases the difficulty of thinking long term.[34]

A second element is the socialization of younger elites, whose educational milieu tends to devalue history and shared national experience. For example, although the American world of higher education is vast, and it would be a mistake to assume that any description applies uniformly, the teaching of the American founding and of diplomatic history has declined precipitously, along with economic, military, and constitutional history. As a case in point, at the University of Wisconsin's prestigious history department, a recent survey found that of forty-five faculty members, only one listed as a specialty diplomatic history and one cited American foreign policy, whereas thirteen named gender, race, or ethnicity as their specialties.[35]

As a rule, general courses on American history and foreign policy continue to be taught, but within a vast menu of course offerings. Fragmentation of the disciplines of history and political science and the emphasis on cutting-edge topics and methodologies are an important part of this shift, as is a pervasive, albeit diffuse, political correctness. To the extent that broader themes are dealt with, they are less likely to

---

[34] The impact of what has been called "the CNN effect" is subject to debate. A thoughtful case study by Matthew A. Baum finds that public scrutiny can inhibit American presidents from using force, especially when the strategic stakes are relatively limited. In addition, it also raises the potential domestic political costs of a bad outcome. See Matthew A. Baum, "How Public Opinion Constrains the Use of Force: The Case of Operation Restore Hope," *Presidential Studies Quarterly*, Vol. 34, No. 2 (June 2004): 187–226.

[35] See, e.g., Patricia Cohen, "Great Caesar's Ghost! Are Traditional History Courses Vanishing?" *The New York Times*, June 11, 2009.

be those of grand strategy and American exceptionalism than concepts of race, class, and gender.[36] There is also a partisan and ideological underlay. Surveys of faculty political preferences show a distinct tilt to the left.[37] For example, an authoritative study of full-time faculty at four-year institutions found 8.8 percent describing themselves as far left, 47 percent as liberal, 28.4 percent as middle of the road, 15.2 percent as conservative, and 0.7 percent as far right. These data illustrate a sharp contrast with the wider public, as evident in a Gallup survey taken during a similar period. Gallup found just 20 percent of Americans describing themselves as liberal, 35 percent as moderate, and 42 percent as conservative.[38] By itself, this ideological imbalance does not necessarily dictate partisanship in teaching and scholarship, although such bias certainly exists. On this subject, Robert Jervis has cautioned about the potential unintended consequences of truncated discourse:

An intriguing complication is that our explanations here may of necessity be strongly influenced by our own policy preferences. The political science profession is dominated by liberal Democrats, which means that most of us feel that the country is harmed by the conservative tendencies that are so powerful now and have operated throughout most of American history. Our preferences may drive us toward explanations involving forms of false consciousness because it is otherwise hard to explain why so many of our compatriots act against what we believe to be their own interests.[39]

---

[36] The American Historical Association (AHA) has released a survey suggesting that emphasis on military and diplomatic history is increasing, but an outside examination of this report finds reason for skepticism. It criticizes the methodology of the survey (which asked professors to list as many as five areas of interest rather than the three previously used), notes that AHA conference programs indicate little presence of these subjects, and cites the "re-visioning" that makes these areas of research "indistinguishable from the dominant race/class/gender paradigm." See K. C. Johnson, "Are Military and Diplomatic History Making a Comeback?" *Mindingthecampus.com*, July 25, 2011, http://www.mindingthecampus.com/forum/2011/07/are_military_and_diplomatic_hi.html, accessed August 18, 2011.

[37] "Opinions and Attitudes of Full-Time Faculty Members, 2007–08, All 4-year Institutions," Source: *The American College Teacher: National Norms, for the 2007–8 HERI Faculty Survey*, UCLA Higher Education Research Institute, in *The Chronicle of Higher Education*, August 28, 2009, pp. 18, 27.

[38] See Lydia Sad, "In 2010, Conservatives Still Outnumber Moderates, Liberals (Princeton, NJ: Gallup, June 25, 2010), http://www.gallup.com/poll/141032/2010-Conservatives-Outnumber-Moderates-Liberals.aspx, accessed August 11, 2010.

[39] Robert Jervis, in "APSA Presidents Reflect on Political Science: Who Knows What, When, and How?" *Perspectives on Politics*, Vol. 3, No. 2 (2005): 309–334, at 316.

There is evidence, especially in the field of history, that unbalanced narratives of the American past are not uncommon. For example, a study of articles about American communism, appearing from 1972 to 2009 in a leading scholarly publication, *The Journal of American History*, found three dozen articles that praised or were sympathetic to American communism or damning of the excesses of anticommunism, but none that were explicitly critical of the party or its followers.[40] Large numbers of students in high school and college have been introduced to American history through the best-selling textbook of the late Howard Zinn, a work that provides an unrelentingly pejorative treatment of America from 1492 to the present, and that reduces the past to what even a respected left-liberal historian describes as a "Manichean fable."[41]

In another subject area, Middle East studies, pervasive biases affect analysis. They reflect the widespread embrace of the ideas of the late Edward Said and of interpretations that focus disproportionately on Western colonialism and imperialism (although the United States was never a colonial power in the region). These approaches downplay or ignore altogether the critical problems identified in the 2002 *Arab Human Development Report*, written for the UN Development Program, citing the Arab world's profound deficits in the treatment of women, in political freedom, and in access to knowledge and information.[42] As a result, the upheavals that in the winter and spring of 2010–2011 shook the Arab world came largely as a surprise to many scholars, intelligence analysts, and policy makers.

A third contemporary element that complicates formulation of a coherent national strategy concerns factors that detract from a sense

And see Robert Lieber, "Sifting and Winnowing: The Uses and Abuses of Academic Freedom," *International Studies Perspectives*, Vol. 8, No. 4 (November 2007): 410–417.

[40] Harvey Klehr and John Earl Haynes, "Revising Revisionism: A New Look at American Communism," *Academic Questions*, Vol. 22, No. 4 (Fall 2009): 452–462, at 461. The period covered is from 1972 until June 2009.

[41] Michael Kazin, "Howard Zinn's History Lessons," *Dissent* (Spring 2004), reviewing *A People's History of the United States, 1492–Present* (New York: Perennial Classics, 2003). The book went through at least five editions and sold more than a million copies.

[42] United Nations Development Program, *Arab Human Development Report 2002*, sponsored by the Regional Bureau for Arab States (New York: UNDP, 2002), http://www.nakbaonline.org/download/UNDP/EnglishVersion/Ar-Human-Dev-2002.pdf.

of national community and shared identity. Those Americans whose formative years took place between the 1930s and the early 1960s lived through such experiences as the Great Depression, World War II, victory over Nazi Germany and Japan, the postwar reintegration of 16 million military veterans, the initial Cold War period, the Marshall Plan, containment of the Soviet Union, the GI Bill, postwar prosperity, the rebuilding of Europe and Japan, the initial idealism of the Kennedy administration, Lyndon Johnson's "Great Society," the passage of civil rights legislation, and the landing of Americans on the moon. To be sure, those years also saw multiple disputes about domestic and foreign policies, ample political strife, a bloody stalemate in the Korean War, and several recessions; but even so, for the great majority of the population, their experiences conveyed a sense that America and its government could be, at least under the right circumstances, both effective and a force for good at home and abroad.

For a successor generation, whose reference points were Vietnam, Watergate, revelations about excesses of the CIA and FBI, two oil shocks, the Iranian embassy hostage crisis, and the troubled presidencies of Lyndon Johnson, Richard Nixon, and Jimmy Carter, government seemed neither effective nor benign. Racial tension, urban riots, student and antiwar movements that metastasized into violence, drugs, the counterculture, a president resigning in disgrace, withdrawal from South Vietnam, inflation, and a severe recession were hallmarks of the period from the late 1960s to the early 1980s.

In addition to these events, there have been underlying social changes that further work against a sense of community and that make shared experiences – for example, in neighborhoods, schools, and the military – less common. Among these defining social changes has been the end of the draft in 1973. The percentage of men who are military veterans or on active duty has declined from 60 percent in the age group 70–79 and 21 percent among those 50–59, to 13 percent for 30–39-year-olds, and to a low of 8 percent in the 18–29-year-old cohort.[43] Other elements of social change include the hollowing out of

---

[43] Frank Newport, "U.S. Military Personnel, Veterans Give Obama Lower Marks," *Gallup.com*, May 30, 2011, http://www.gallup.com/poll/147839/Military-Personnel-Veterans-Give-Obama-Lower-Marks.aspx, accessed June 23, 2011. The percentage for women has been increasing but remains in the low single digits.

numerous central cities and the flight of many whites and middle-class blacks to more distant suburbs, the crisis in urban public education, and a growing distrust of authority in private and public institutions.

In recent decades, polarization among political elites has intensified, as evidenced in Congress, where there are far fewer liberal Republicans and conservative Democrats, and where cross-cutting cleavages have become less common. Indeed, an authoritative study of political distance between the parties from 1879 to 2009 finds that the average positions of Democratic and Republican legislators have been diverging markedly since the mid-1970s, and that "[p]olarization in the House and Senate is now at the highest level since the end of Reconstruction."[44]

Although the violence and disorder of an earlier era have not been repeated, bitter divisions over the Clinton impeachment in 1998–1999, the contested 2000 presidential election of George W. Bush, the Iraq War, and responses to the financial and economic crises of 2008–2011 have all left their mark. Governmental competence has been called into question, too, as in reaction to Hurricane Katrina in September 2005 and the BP-Deepwater Horizon oil spill in the Gulf of Mexico in April–May 2010. Beliefs and ideas about America's place in the world also have an impact. Among liberal internationalists, attachment to international institutions and the UN has for many become a predominant value. From this perspective, there is often unease or discomfort about American exceptionalism and power, along with a belief that the exercise of power may be illegitimate unless it carries the imprimatur of the UN Security Council or another major multilateral institution. Meanwhile, among a minority current on the political right, isolationism and ultra-libertarianism also run counter to a sense of shared national community.

The connections of these ideas, trends, and experiences to strategy and foreign policy are diffuse and indirect, but they condition an atmosphere in which it is harder to summon a sense of nationhood and to seek or reach consensus about America's world role. However,

[44] Nolan McCarty, Keith T. Poole, and Howard Rosenthal, *Polarized America: The Dance of Ideology and Unequal Riches* (Cambridge, MA: MIT Press, 2006), and "Party Polarization: 1879–2009," updated January 11, 2011, http:// polarizedamerica.com/#POLITICALPOLARIZATION, accessed April 8, 2011.

partisanship and ideological divisions run much deeper among political elites and members of Congress than the public as a whole. While the phenomenon of partisan "sorting" has been taking place, so that those who consider themselves liberals or conservatives have for some two decades been gravitating to the "correct" political party, partisan ideologues remain a distinct minority. In this regard, Morris Fiorina, a leading scholar of American politics, observes: "For the most part Americans continue to be ambivalent, moderate, and pragmatic, in contrast to the cocksure extremists and ideologues who dominate our public life."[45] Moreover, Fiorina finds that claims about cultural and social polarization have also been exaggerated:

The simple truth is that there is no cultural war in the United States.... Many of the activists in the political parties and the various cause groups do, in fact, hate each other and regard themselves as combatants in a war. But their hatreds and battles are not shared by the great mass of the American people... who are for the most part moderate in their views and tolerant in their manner.[46]

Evidence from voting results and public opinion surveys reflects these patterns. For example, when the 112th Congress convened in January 2011 following big Republican gains in the November 2010 elections, large majorities of Americans expressed their desire for both parties to work together. A Gallup Poll found that 90 percent of Democrats and 77 percent of Republicans said it was "extremely" or "very" important that Republican and Democratic leaders work with President Obama to pass new legislation that both parties could agree on.[47]

The impact on foreign policy can be oblique, but statements and speeches of policy makers suggest that these competing beliefs about the exercise of American power are very real. To cite a contemporary example, President Barack Obama in his statements about foreign policy downplayed the relevance or importance of American exceptionalism. In a widely quoted response to a reporter's question, he

---

[45] Morris P. Fiorina, with Samuel J. Adams and Jeremy C. Pope, *Culture War? The Myth of a Polarized America* (New York: Longman, 3rd ed., 2011), p. xiii.

[46] Ibid., p. 8.

[47] "Americans Strongly Desire That Political Leaders Work Together," *Gallup.com*, January 19, 2011, http://www.gallup.com/poll/145679/Americans-Strongly-Desire-Political-Leaders-Work-Together.aspx?version=print, accessed April 11, 2011.

replied, "I believe in American exceptionalism, just as I suspect that the Brits believe in British exceptionalism and the Greeks believe in Greek exceptionalism."[48] The 2010 *National Security Strategy* (NSS) exhibited some of this diffidence, although it also included passages about the importance of American military might. Thus, on the one hand, it contained wording that would not have been out of place at any time during the previous seven decades: "This Administration has no greater responsibility than protecting the American people. Furthermore, we embrace America's unique responsibility to promote international security – a responsibility that flows from our commitments to allies, our leading role in supporting a just and sustainable international order, and our unmatched military capabilities."[49] On the other hand, the Obama NSS also incorporated more ambivalent language. While it called for "defeating al-Qaeda and its affiliates," it referred throughout to "violent extremists" but never once in the entire fifty-two-page document to jihadism or radical Islamism. The unwillingness to describe accurately the movement and ideology that poses a serious threat to the United States, its interests, and allies, as well as to Muslim communities in which radical Islamism contends for power, represented a striking omission. Contrast this not only with the 2002 and 2006 National Security Strategy documents, but also with the language of the bipartisan 9/11 Commission report, which unambiguously stated: "The catastrophic threat at this moment in history is more specific. It is the threat posed by *Islamist* terrorism – especially the al Qaeda network, its affiliates, and its ideology."[50]

The 2010 NSS also emphasized international institutions in expansive language that gave lip service to their shortcomings, but it did not come to grips with their limitations in confronting the most urgent problems and perils:

We will expand our support to modernizing institutions and arrangements such as the evolution of the G-8 to the G-20 to reflect the realities of today's

---

[48] President Obama's response to a reporter's question at the G-20 Summit, Strasbourg, France, April 4, 2009. Quoted in James Kirchick, "Squanderer in Chief," *Los Angeles Times*, April 28, 2009.

[49] *National Security Strategy* (Washington, DC: U.S. Government Printing Office, May 2010), p. 17, http://www.whitehouse.gov/sites/default/files/rss_viewer/national_security_strategy.pdf

[50] *The 9/11 Commission Report: Final Report of the National Commission on Terrorist Attacks Upon the United States* (New York: W. W. Norton, 2004), p. 362.

international environment. Working with the institutions and the countries that comprise them, we will enhance international capacity to prevent conflict, spur economic growth, improve security, combat climate change, and address the challenges posed by weak and failing states. And we will challenge and assist international institutions and frameworks to reform when they fail to live up to their promise. Strengthening the legitimacy and authority of international law and institutions, especially the U.N., will require a constant struggle to improve performance.[51]

In practice, ideas and preconceptions tend to be mitigated by the pressure of events. This was evident, for example, by the way in which the Obama administration adapted to circumstances in Iraq and Afghanistan. Subsequently, the decision to intervene in Libya reflected competing imperatives inside the administration, with the president and his principal foreign policy officials initially reluctant to see the United States drawn in. Worsening circumstances on the ground and especially agreement by the Arab League, the UN Security Council, and NATO provided the multilateral legitimization that had become a sine qua non for Obama administration policy makers. Initially, the president's expressed objective that Qaddafi must go appeared inconsistent with the stated means: protection of civilians and transferring responsibility to NATO, rather than a commitment to direct military operations for the explicit purpose of ousting the Libyan leader. One of Obama's advisors later described the President's actions in Libya as "leading from behind."[52]

"Will versus Wallet" in the American Future

Debate about America's world role is nothing new. One notable version of it took place in the late 1980s. Paul Kennedy's 1987 best seller, *The Rise and Fall of the Great Powers*, became one of the most widely cited books of that era. Kennedy cautioned that the United States ran the risk of "imperial overstretch," which he defined not just in terms of military commitments, but in regard to the balance between resources and obligations.[53] In a 1990 response, Joseph Nye was less pessimistic,

---

[51] *National Security Strategy* (2010), p. 13.
[52] Quoted in Ryan Lizza, "The Consequentialist: How the Arab Spring Remade Obama's Foreign Policy," *The New Yorker*, May 2, 2011.
[53] Paul Kennedy, *The Rise and Fall of the Great Powers: Economic Change and Military Conflict from 1500 to 2000* (New York: Random, 1987).

arguing that the issue was not one of resources per se, but of policy and choice – that is, that to the extent the United States faced a problem, it was because it "lacks the will, not the wallet."[54]

The problem of "wallet" has since become more pressing. Even before the financial crisis that began in 2008, the historian Niall Ferguson cited the shift in America's balance of payments and the change in its net international investment position – the difference between American-owned assets abroad and foreign-owned American assets – as a sign of deterioration. In doing so, he invoked comparisons with the decline and fall of the Roman Empire nearly two millennia ago.[55] The comparison is tempting, but as with the parallels to the British experience of the past century, its relevance is tenuous at best.

More importantly, does the scale and nature of challenges abroad together with the weight of problems at home mean that the United States no longer has the capacity to play a leading role in world affairs, or is it the case that domestic perceptions, beliefs, and policy choices are as much or more at issue? In short, does the United States still possess the necessary resources – the "wallet" – and does it retain the "will"? Is the declinist proposition valid, that, as a society, economy, and political power, the country is in decline? Certainly the domestic situation is more difficult now than two decades ago. Yet while these problems should not be minimized, they should not be overstated either. Contrary to what many observers would assume, the United States has managed to hold its own in globalized economic competition and its strengths remain broad and deep. For the past several decades, its share of global output has been relatively constant at between one-quarter and one-fifth of world output. According to data from the International Monetary Fund (IMF), in 1980, the United States accounted for 26.0 percent of world GDP, and in 2011, 21.5 percent. These figures are based on GDP in national currency. Alternative calculations using purchasing power parities are somewhat less

---

[54] Joseph S. Nye, "Is the U.S. Declining? Reply to Paul Kennedy," *The New York Review of Books*, October 11, 1990, and Kennedy's rejoinder. Also see Joseph S. Nye, *Bound to Lead: The Changing Nature of American Power* (New York: Basic Books, 1990).

[55] Niall Ferguson, "Empire Falls," *Vanity Fair*, October 2006.

favorable, but still show the United States with 19.1 percent in 2011, as contrasted with 24.6 percent in 1980.[56]

Moreover, America benefits from a growing population and one that is aging more slowly than all its possible competitors except India. And despite a dysfunctional immigration system, it continues to be a magnet for talented and ambitious immigrants. It is a world leader in science and in its system of research universities and higher education, and it has the advantage of continental scale and resources. In short, the United States remains the one country in the world that is both big and rich.[57]

In addition, the American military remains unmatched and, despite intense stress from a decade of war in Afghanistan and Iraq, it has not suffered the disarray that afflicted it in Vietnam. This is evident in terms of indicators such as successful recruitment and performance of the volunteer force, the ongoing quality of the officer corps, and broad public support for the military as well as casualty tolerance. Moreover, in its capabilities, technology, capacity to project power, and command of the global commons, the United States has actually increased its military margin as compared with others, although with the important and challenging exception of China.

Beyond material strengths, the society itself benefits from a durable political system, rule of law, vigorous free press and information media, and a competitive and adaptable economy, as well as strong traditions of entrepreneurship and innovation, leadership and critical mass in new technology, and a history of resilience and flexibility in overcoming adversity.

The declinist proposition that America's international primacy is collapsing as a result of the rise of other countries should also be regarded with caution. On the one hand, the United States does face a more competitive world, regional challenges, and some attrition of its relative degree of primacy. This process, or diffusion of power, is not exclusive to the post–Cold War era, but began at least four decades

---

[56] Source: *World Economic Outlook Database.* International Monetary Fund. October 2010, http://www.imf.org/external/pubs/ft/weo/2011/02/weodata/index.aspx, accessed October 29, 2011.

[57] William C. Wohlforth has made a similar point, e.g., "Unipolarity, Status Competition, and Great Power War," *World Politics*, Vol. 61, No. 1 (January 2009): 28–57.

ago with the recovery of Europe and Japan from World War II, the rise of the Soviet Union to superpower status, and the emergence of regional powers in Asia, Latin America, the Middle East, and Africa.[58] Still, in contrast to other great powers that have experienced decline, the United States has held a substantially more dominant position. For example, Britain at the start of the twentieth century was already falling behind Germany and the United States, although it did manage to continue for half a century as head of a vast empire and commonwealth.

Because of the enormous margin of power the United States possessed after the end of the Cold War, it should be able to withstand erosion in its relative strength for some time to come without losing its predominant status. While it is true that the weight of important regional powers has increased, many of these are allied or friendly. Those that are not (Iran, North Korea, Syria, and Venezuela) do not by themselves constitute serious balancing against the United States and its allies. Russia occupies an intermediate position, at times acting as a spoiler, but not an outright adversary. China presents a potentially more formidable challenge, notably through its growing economic might and the rapid expansion of its military capacity, but it has not yet become a true peer competitor. In any case, and despite the burden of a decade of war in the Middle East, America continues to possess significant advantages in economic breadth and depth, science, technology, competitiveness, demography, force size, power projection, military technology, and even in learning how to carry out effective counterinsurgency, and thus retains the capacity to meet key objectives.

In sum, although the United States predominates by lesser margins, it still remains a long way from being overtaken by peer competitors. However, given profound disagreements about policy, intense partisan rancor among political elites, growing social-class division, distrust of government, and deep disagreement about foreign commitments, nonmaterial factors could prove to be a greater impediment

---

[58] Kenneth Oye and I emphasized the effects of the diffusion of power in Kenneth A. Oye, Donald Rothchild, and Robert J. Lieber (eds.), *Eagle Entangled: U.S. Foreign Policy in a Complex World* (New York: Longman, 1979); and Oye, Lieber, and Rothchild (eds.), *Eagle Defiant: U.S. Foreign Policy in the 1980s* (Boston: Little, Brown, 1983).

to staying power than more commonly cited indicators of economic problems and military overstretch. Can the American political system produce effective measures to cope with long-term burdens of entitlement programs and national debt? Will cultural and generational differences about the uses and even legitimacy of American power lead to abandonment of a global leadership role? And are persistent foreign threats, especially from terrorism and nuclear proliferation, likely to sustain a domestic consensus or instead lead to intensified polarization and retrenchment? The United States retains the power and capacity to play a leading world role. The ultimate questions about America's future are likely to be those of policy and will.

2

Domestic and Global Interactions

Economics, Energy, and American Power

"Why should [Westerners] fear China? . . . I believe the Americans will always have the advantage because of their all-embracive society, and the English language that makes it easy to attract foreign talent."
— Lee Kuan Yew (former Singapore prime minister)[1]

The financial crisis and recession of the past few years have seriously strained the American economy and thus the capacity of the United States to play its accustomed international role. Unprecedented annual budget deficits, a steep trajectory for the costs of entitlement and health care programs, and soaring increases in the national debt pose severe challenges. As a proportion of the overall economy, deficits in the federal budget as well as the total federal debt have reached their highest levels since the end of World War II. According to a widely cited estimate by the Congressional Budget Office (CBO), and assuming current policies continue, public debt would reach nearly 90 percent of GDP by the year 2020, leading the Director of the CBO to warn that federal debt could grow to "unsustainable levels."[2]

If these imbalances cannot be brought under control, they are likely to lead to demands for the curtailment of military, financial, and

---

[1] Quoted in Patrick Barta and Robert Thomas, "Lee Kuan Yew: The World Needs a Strong U.S.," *The Wall Street Journal*, April 26, 2011.

[2] Douglas W. Elmendorf, Director, in preface to *The Long-Term Budget Outlook* (Washington, DC: Congressional Budget Office, Congress of the United States, June 2010). Data cited here are from the Summary and Chapter One of the Report.

political commitments abroad. As an early hint of such pressures, the Chair of the Senate Appropriations Committee cited "severe economic difficulties facing our nation," in imposing a modest cut of $2.6 billion from a presidential international affairs budget request (that is, non-defense foreign policy spending).[3] A much more concrete sign was the legislation of August 2, 2011, to raise the national debt ceiling, painfully hammered out in negotiations between the White House and Republicans in Congress. The agreement authorized nearly $1 trillion in spending reductions over a period of ten years. None of these cuts were to affect defense, law enforcement, or scientific research. However, the Obama administration and the Department of Defense had already committed to cutting some $400 billion from the defense budget over the next decade. Moreover, after the failure in November 2011 of a bipartisan congressional "supercommittee" to reach agreement on an additional $1.5 trillion of deficit reduction, automatic decreases of that amount were to be triggered in 2013, of which half was to come from defense and the remainder from other discretionary spending. If actually implemented, these sweeping across-the-board cuts would be bound to have a significant impact on America's foreign and security policy role.

The impact of the financial problem was vividly symbolized for many Americans when, just three days after the debt ceiling agreement, the rating firm Standard & Poor's took the unprecedented step of downgrading America's long-term credit rating from AAA to AA-plus. Yet as serious as these problems of debt and deficit have become, they are a relatively recent phenomenon. Much of this surge in the national debt has occurred over a relatively short period. Over most of the prior forty years and until the early part of the past decade, it had averaged only 36 percent of GDP, and as late as the end of 2008, the debt amounted to just 40 percent.

---

[3] Sen. Daniel Inouye (D-Hawaii) citing a cut in the $56.7 billion budget request for the 2011 fiscal year. Chairman Inouye Opening Statement at July 15 Full Committee Markup, U.S. Senate Committee on Appropriations, Washington, DC, July 15, 2010, http://appropriations.senate.gov/news.cfm?method=news.view&id=567dffbd-691b-40d6-a210-c512322cf023, accessed July 19, 2010. Actual international affairs spending totaled $55 billion in fiscal 2010 and $49 billion in FY 2011. Stephen Lee Myers, "Foreign Aid Faces Major Cutbacks in Budget Crisis," *New York Times*, October 4, 2011.

The economic and financial pressures that have combined to cause the deficit in its current and projected dimensions are a product of multiple sources. The long and costly wars in Afghanistan and Iraq, together with other global war on terror operations, led to expenditures of more than $1.1 trillion in the decade after 9/11.[4] This is an enormous sum, including $140 billion in 2010 alone, but in the context of a $14 trillion GDP and a $3.5 trillion annual budget, it has been accompanied or even surpassed by three other major causes.

The first of these sources of growing deficit and debt is the increasing structural gap between taxes and federal government expenditures. Large tax cuts in 2001 and 2003 and a major prescription drug benefit in 2006 were passed with bipartisan support in the Congress and signed by President George W. Bush. These measures were put in place without offsetting spending controls or revenue enhancements and have resulted in major additions to the deficit.

Second, there have been the effects of the domestic and then global financial crisis. This began in late 2007 with the bursting of the U.S. real estate bubble. There followed in the fall of 2008 an unprecedented credit crisis triggered by the collapse of Lehman Brothers and in 2009 the subsequent "Great Recession." The federal response to these crises took the form of emergency measures including costly bailouts of the banking and insurance sectors, the auto industry, and housing. Among these, the ongoing expense of supporting the mortgage giants Fannie Mae and Freddie Mac has amounted to hundreds of billions of dollars. Together with a $787 billion stimulus bill, these measures have added to unprecedented annual budget deficits.

Third, the greatest long-term burden is that of entitlements. The gradual aging of the American population, though less pronounced than in Western Europe, Japan, Russia, or China, will have momentous consequences. The retirement of the Baby Boom generation (those born in the two decades after World War II) will mean an enormous increase in payments for Social Security, Medicare, Medicaid, and veterans' benefits. These programs for older Americans already amount to almost half of non-interest federal spending, and in just fifteen years,

---

[4] *The Cost of Iraq, Afghanistan, and Other Global War on Terror Operations since 9/11* (Washington, DC: Congressional Research Service), September 28, 2009. The estimate covers the period from 9/11 through the 2010 fiscal year.

from 2010 to 2025, the number of those enrolled in Social Security and Medicare will grow by 50 percent.[5] Added to these expenditures are the growing costs for medical care in legislation passed in 2010, the Patient Protection and Affordable Care Act (PPACA), also known as ObamaCare.

Together, these factors have caused annual deficits to surge in recent years. From 2009 through 2011, budget deficits averaged between 9 percent and 10 percent of GDP, and the projected gap between federal revenues and expenditures threatens to become unsustainable. This represents a striking contrast with the record of the previous several decades, where from the beginning of the 1970s, spending by the federal government had averaged 21 percent of GDP, while tax revenue averaged 18 percent. As the nonpartisan Congressional Budget office has warned, even if revenues recover from the effects of recession and remain close to their historic average percentage of GDP, the rise in spending for entitlements will cause rapid increases in deficits and federal debt. Thus, if the federal debt is to be prevented from becoming unsupportable, policy makers will have to restrain spending growth, raise revenue, or adopt some combination of the two.[6] (See Table 2.1, Total Revenues and Outlays, 1971–2021.)

As part of the effort to cope with these costs, spending on foreign policy is likely to become a conspicuous target for deficit reduction. The defense budget, the stationing of troops abroad, intelligence agencies, foreign aid, contributions to international organizations, and decisions about foreign intervention will be subject to intense scrutiny. Christopher Layne, a scholarly critic of America's expansive foreign policy, contends that trillion-dollar deficits for a decade or more and "an increasingly unsustainable and urgent fiscal problem" mean that in contrast to its long-standing role as a hegemon, "The United States no longer fits the part."[7] Similarly, Michael Mandelbaum argues that

---

[5] In 2010, these programs represented $1.6 trillion of the $3.3 trillion in federal non-interest spending. Robert Samuelson, "Why We're in the Soup," *realclear-politics.com*, July 11, 2011, http://www.realclearpolitics.com/articles/2011/07/11/why_were_in_the_soup_110515.html, accessed August 19, 2011.

[6] Congressional Budget Office, *The Budget and Economic Outlook: Fiscal years 2011 to 2021*, January 2011, http://www.cbo.gov/ftpdocs/120xx/doc12039/SummaryforWeb.pdf, accessed June 28, 2011.

[7] Christopher Layne, "Graceful Decline: The End of Pax Americana," *The American Conservative*, April 6, 2010, pp. 30–31.

TABLE 2.1. *Total Revenues and Outlays, 1971–2021*

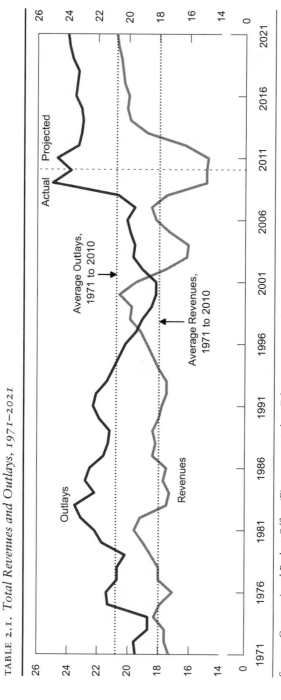

Source: Congressional Budget Office. (Figure corrected on February 15, 2011.) *The Budget and Economic Outlook: Fiscal years 2011 to 2021,* January 2011 http://www.cbo.gov/ftpdocs/120xx/doc12039/SummaryforWeb.pdf

because of the intensifying pressure to choose between guns and butter, domestic obligations will narrow the scope of foreign policy. As a result, he anticipates that, "In the future, the United States will behave more like an ordinary country."[8]

Another source of pressure results from the squeeze on discretionary spending in the federal budget. As entitlement programs have grown, the share of the federal budget available for all its other activities is increasingly constricted. As a result, defense spending becomes a target not only because of the huge sums it represents, but because defense as a whole makes up approximately 53 percent of discretionary outlays, that is, the share of the federal budget not already legally obligated for programs such as Medicare, Medicaid, Social Security, veterans' benefits, and interest on the debt.[9] Under these circumstances, the fact that defense as a proportion of GDP (approximately 4.9 percent, including the cost of Afghanistan and Iraq) is modest compared with averages over the past six decades can be overshadowed by the reality that it represents the largest single programmatic area in which there is a possibility of meaningful spending cuts.

In turn, the nonmilitary components of foreign policy represent a much smaller fraction of U.S. government spending. The entire international affairs budget – for diplomacy, international broadcasting, international institutions, humanitarian assistance, and foreign aid – amounts to approximately $49 billion, or less than 4 percent of discretionary spending. The portion devoted to foreign aid has long been a target for reductions and at times has been less popular with the American public than expenditures for domestic welfare payments. The quintessential criticism on this subject was expressed with the quip that if you are not happy about welfare payments here at home, you should be even more critical of welfare abroad. Reports of massive inefficiency and corruption in the aid programs for Iraq and Afghanistan have intensified these critiques as well as public skepticism. Outside these regions, however, the sums committed to foreign aid are

---

[8] Michael Mandelbaum, *The Frugal Superpower: America's Global Leadership in a Cash-Strapped Era* (New York: PublicAffairs, 2010), p. 8.
[9] Author's calculation based on CBO baseline projections for 2012, discretionary outlays of $1,352 billion, with defense outlays of $710 billion. See *The Budget and Economic Outlook: Fiscal years 2011 to 2021*, Table 3.9, "Projections of Discretionary Spending Under Selected Policy Alternatives," p. 82.

relatively modest in size, amounting to less than 1 percent of the federal budget and 0.2 percent of GDP.

As compelling as these and many similar assessments may be concerning the economic pressures for retrenchment, a seriously diminished American world role is avoidable. To be sure, the financial dangers are real, especially debt projections unprecedented for an era in which the United States is not embroiled in a major war, and these burdens require far-reaching policy responses. However, while they create a *propensity* toward foreign policy retrenchment, this result is by no means a certainty.

Financial Crises in Perspective

Historical comparisons suggest that the United States has the capacity to surmount challenges far more daunting than those posed by contemporary financial constraints. Among the most important cases are the Civil War, the Depression of the 1930s, World War II, and the Cold War. Even if we compare only past financial crises with the current period of economic trouble, there is reason for encouragement, although not for complacency. The American experience over the past two centuries includes financial panics and recessions, sometimes quite severe, in almost every generation. The historical record is replete with speculative bubbles, stock market and real estate failures, widespread bankruptcies, periods of high unemployment, and crises in banking, credit, and insurance. These cases are also worth recalling not only as a reminder of the severe disruptions that can occur, but also of the resilience of the American economy and society, often in the face of intensely pessimistic assessments and forecasts.

For example, during the course of the nineteenth century, as the United States grew from its original thirteen colonies and expanded across the entire continent to become a major power, the country experienced several financial upheavals. Those with the greatest impact included five such crises in a period of seventy-five years:

- 1819–1821, financial panic and recession. Bank failures, foreclosures, economic hardship.
- 1836–1842, financial panic and recession. British and U.S. speculation in cotton, textiles, railroads, and land led to banking and

real estate collapses; severe hardship in farming and rural areas worsened by crop failure.

- 1857–1859, financial panic and recession. Stock market crash, collapse of major insurance firms, massive bankruptcies in the financial sector.
- 1861–1876, Civil War and Reconstruction. Enormous costs of war in men and material. Devastation of the South's major cities and its nascent industries.
- 1893–1897, financial panic and depression. The worst economic crisis prior to the Great Depression of the 1930s. Stock market crash, credit crisis, high unemployment.[10]

These nineteenth-century crises show that downturns and recoveries are not new, although apart from the Civil War, the United States did not bear the financial burdens of maintaining a major global role or of entitlement spending.

Twentieth-century crises are more familiar, most notably the Great Depression, triggered by the 1929 stock market crash and lasting throughout the following decade. The era saw widespread foreclosures, bank failures, agricultural collapse, and the ravages of the Dust Bowl. In January 1937, in his second inaugural address, President Franklin Roosevelt gave voice to a widespread concern about the condition of one-third of a nation, "ill-clothed, ill-housed, and ill-nourished." At the nadir of the Depression, a quarter of the American workforce was unemployed, and the country did not emerge from its economic crisis until World War II. The experience left a deep and lasting impression on American society, but what is especially relevant about the era is that at the time it gave rise to widespread pessimism about the

---

[10] Sources: Murray N. Rothbard, *The Panic of 1819: Reactions and Policies* (New York: Columbia University Press, 1962), pp. 16, 18, 28; Willard L. Thorp, *Business Annals* (New York: National Bureau of Economic Research, 1926), pp. 118–128, 136–137; James F. Rhodes, *History of the United States From the Compromise of 1850* (New York: Harper & Brothers, 1900), pp. 44–48; Paul P. Paskoff, "Measures of War: A Quantitative Examination of the Civil War's Destructiveness in the Confederacy," *Civil War History*, Vol. 54, No. 1: 37–40; Samuel Rezneck, "Unemployment, Unrest, and Relief in the United States during the Depression of 1893–1897," *The Journal of Political Economy*, Vol. 61, No. 4: 333–338; Charles P. Kindleberger, *Manias, Panics, and Crashes: A History of Financial Crises* (New York: Basic Books, 1978); Carmen M. Reinhart and Kenneth S. Rogoff, *This Time Is Different: Eight Centuries of Financial Folly* (Princeton: Princeton University Press, 2009).

American future. Together with the severe economic, social, and political turmoil affecting Europe during the same period and the rise of
communist and fascist regimes there (the Soviet Union, Fascist Italy,
Nazi Germany), many began to question or even to despair about
whether the American model of liberal democracy and the market
economy was any longer viable.

Following the end of World War II, America benefitted from
strong economic performance, with impressive expansion in economic
growth, employment, productivity, innovation, population, and living
standards, although the record also included periods of real economic
difficulty – together with accompanying bouts of pessimism about the
American future. Smaller recessions have not been unusual (recessions
being defined as at least two consecutive calendar quarters of negative
economic growth).[11]

Past concerns were by no means only about the economy. The
successful Soviet launch of the Sputnik space satellite in October 1957 –
the first man-made object ever to leave earth's atmosphere and achieve
orbit – led to questions about whether the United States was falling
seriously behind in science, technology, and the space race. At the time,
it was argued that in contrast to the centrally directed state economy of
the USSR, America with its consumer-oriented market economy was
lagging in the education of its youth, especially in math and science.
Coupled with a sharp recession in 1957–1958, this experience provided
both the impetus for the subsequent pledge of presidential candidate
John F. Kennedy to "get America moving again" and for a major
expansion of higher education.

Two recessions in the 1970s were the most severe of the Cold War
era. The oil crisis, triggered by the October 1973 Middle East war
and Arab oil embargo and marked by high inflation, recession, and
9 percent unemployment in 1974–1975, seemed to mark an end to
nearly three decades of sustained economic growth and prosperity.
Near the end of the decade, the Iranian revolution, in December 1978–
January 1979, led to the collapse of oil production there and a second oil shock. The reverberations were felt in a severe and prolonged
recession and inflation. The period saw Jimmy Carter's controversial

---

[11] The definition is that of the National Bureau of Economic Research, a respected
nongovernmental body.

address to the nation in July 1979, widely dubbed the "malaise" speech – although he never actually used the word. In it, the president spoke at length of a crisis in which "[t]he erosion of our confidence in the future is threatening to destroy the social and the political fabric of America," and adding, "The symptoms of this crisis of the American spirit are all around us."[12]

This recession, the worst of the entire postwar period, continued into the early 1980s. It contributed to Carter's defeat by Ronald Reagan in the 1980 presidential election. And in the first year and a half of Reagan's term, interest rates soared to almost 19 percent as the Federal Reserve under Chairman Paul Volker sought to bring inflation under control.[13] In turn, unemployment peaked at 10.8 percent in late 1982.

These experiences and a growing trade gap fostered hyperbolic statements about American decline and the rise of an increasingly unified Europe and an economically dynamic and competitive Japan. The choice of language in these years is quite striking, both for what it conveys about a sense that America was falling behind at the end of the 1970s and into the 1980s, and also about the rise of a formidable Asian peer competitor. Even so, the years from the early 1980s through the end of the 1990s saw impressive American economic performance that outpaced not only Europe but also Japan in job creation, productivity, and economic growth. From today's perspective, with Japan continuing to experience serious economic, social, and political stagnation, the warnings by prominent businessmen, public intellectuals, and scholars of that earlier era appear grossly overstated:

To expect Americans, who are accustomed to thinking of their nation as number one, to acknowledge that in many areas its supremacy has been lost

---

[12] The text of Carter's nationally televised address, delivered July 15, 1979, is available at http://www2.volstate.edu/geades/FinalDocs/1970s&beyond/malaise.htm, accessed July 5, 2011. Reaction to the speech among political elites was widely critical, especially in characterizing President Carter as having blamed the public for a loss of confidence rather than focusing on the policies and problems of his own administration.

[13] The average prime rate peaked at 18.87% in 1981. Data from U.S. Federal Reserve. Average prime rate charged by banks on short-term loans to business, quoted on an investment basis. Rate posted by a majority of top twenty-five insured U.S.-chartered commercial banks. http://www.federalreserve.gov/releases/H15/data/Annual/H15_PRIME_NA.txt, accessed August 20, 2010.

to an Asian nation...is to ask a good deal. – Ezra Vogel, *Japan as Number One* (1979)[14]

Japan is fast becoming the world's leading economic power.... There has been no previous example of the transfer of economic power as rapid as the one now taking place. – George Soros, 1987[15]

This development is epochal.... Japan...now controls the source of wealth and others must come to it as they came to the United States in the past. – Clyde V. Prestowitz, Jr., *Trading Places: How We are Giving our Future to Japan and How We Should Reclaim It* (1988)[16]

With the passage of time, these words sound needlessly pessimistic about the American future. To be sure, the competitive pressure now generated by the economic and political rise of China is of a different order of magnitude and may not be so conveniently overcome, but the earlier experiences should provide a cautionary lesson about such forecasts. This is not only a question of whether the rise of China is sustainable, but also of America's own strengths, adaptability, and leadership.

Competitiveness and Crisis Response

During the first decade of the twenty-first century, the U.S. economy seriously lagged behind its previous performance, growing by an average annual rate of just 1.9 percent. This contrasts with the record of the prior six decades, in which growth had averaged 3.9 percent per year.[17] Despite this record and the intensified pressures of recent years, the United States retains a strong domestic foundation. Based on International Monetary Fund (IMF) data, America's share of world GDP amounts to approximately one-fifth of the world total. Measured at market exchange rates, the figure for 2011 was 21.5 percent, only modestly below the 26.0 percent share it held in 1980. Even calculated with the less favorable comparison based on purchasing power parity,

[14] Quoted, "What the Experts Said," *The Washington Post*, March 30, 1997.
[15] George Soros, "A Global New Deal, *The New York Review of Books*, August 13, 1987.
[16] Quoted, "What the Experts Said," *The Washington Post*, March 30, 1997.
[17] Data from Christopher Wood, CLSA investment group, Hong Kong, cited in "Back to the Crash," *The Economist*, February 27, 2010, p. 36.

the United States accounts for 19.1 percent of the world total GDP, as against 24.6 percent in 1980.[18] (See Tables 2.2 and 2.3)

More important than total GDP are the figures for per capita GDP, a category in which the United States remains well ahead of other major countries. Notably, America's GDP per capita is far above China's and will remain so for a very long time. Although projections by the IMF and others show China likely to overtake America in total GDP (as measured in PPP) as early as 2016, per capita GDP provides a much more robust indicator of national power. China's GDP is large because its population is almost five times that of the United States. But China's per capita GDP is only $9,204 per person whereas that of the United States is $49,055.[19] Moreover, half of China's population is rural and quite poor. What matters most and is made possible by its high GDP per capita is America's overall level of economic development, advanced education, innovation, R&D, advanced technology, military capacity, and other comparable sectors in which it enjoys a substantial edge. Michael Beckley makes an important historical point here by drawing on a nineteenth-century comparison. In 1870, China and India possessed the world's largest economies in GDP terms, yet at that very time China was being humiliated by Western powers and Japan, while India was a British colony. Britain's GDP was then roughly half the size of China's and India's, yet its per capita GDP far surpassed theirs, while it ruled the high seas and presided over an empire covering a fourth of the world.[20]

In terms of world manufacturing production, the U.S. share is estimated at between 17 percent and 20 percent, a proportion of world output only moderately less than four decades ago. According to UN data, in 1978, America accounted for 22.2 percent of world manufacturing, with the figure remaining relatively steady over the following quarter century, so that by 2003 it represented 23.6 percent of the total.

[18] Source: *World Economic Outlook Database*, International Monetary Fund, September 2011, http://www.imf.org/external/pubs/ft/weo/2010/02/weodata/index.aspx, accessed October 29, 2011.

[19] Data on per capita GDP for 2012 from *World Economic Outlook Database*. International Monetary Fund. September 2011, http://www.imf.org/external/pubs/ft/weo/2011/02/weodata/index.aspx. Accessed 29 November 2011.

[20] See Michael Beckley, "China's Century?" *International Security*, Vol. 36, No. 3 (Winter 2011/12), forthcoming.

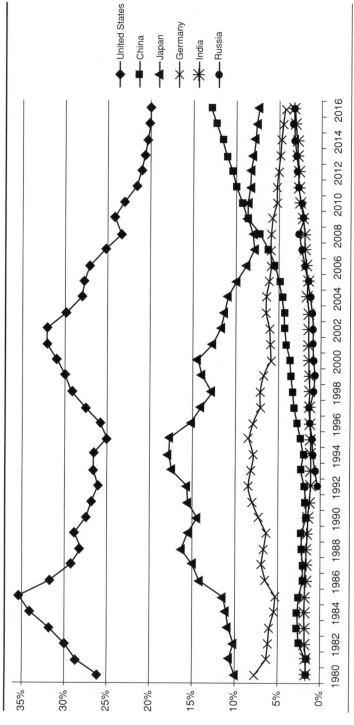

TABLE 2.2. *Percent of World GDP (Market Exchange Rates), 1980–2016*

United States
China
Japan
Germany
India
Russia

Source: Adapted from data in *World Economic Outlook Database.* International Monetary Fund. September 2011. Accessed 29 October 2011. http://www.imf.org/external/pubs/ft/weo/2011/02/weodata/index.aspx

TABLE 2.2 *(continued)*

	1980	1981	1982	1983	1984	1985	1986	1987	1988	1989	1990	1991	1992	1993	1994	1995	1996	1997
United States	26.03	28.59	30.01	31.84	34.07	35.28	31.68	29.31	28.13	28.77	27.37	26.69	26.08	26.72	26.46	24.95	25.74	27.48
China	1.89	1.54	2.60	2.72	2.69	2.57	2.11	2.00	2.23	2.37	1.84	1.82	2.01	2.46	2.09	2.45	2.81	3.14
Japan	10.00	10.82	10.15	10.81	11.06	11.41	14.35	15.15	16.38	15.60	14.43	15.52	15.61	17.43	17.85	17.71	15.24	14.05
Germany	7.71	6.35	6.19	6.03	5.47	5.35	6.49	7.03	6.76	6.39	7.30	8.08	8.51	8.05	8.04	8.50	8.00	7.12
India	1.69	1.79	1.87	1.97	1.91	1.91	1.78	1.71	1.67	1.57	1.53	1.28	1.19	1.14	1.20	1.23	1.24	1.39
Russia	n/a	n/a	n/a	n/a	n/a	n/a	n/a	n/a	n/a	n/a	n/a	n/a	0.35	0.74	1.03	1.05	1.29	1.34

	1998	1999	2000	2001	2002	2003	2004	2005	2006	2007	2008	2009	2010	2011	2012	2013	2014	2015	2016
United States	29.23	29.93	30.89	32.14	31.98	29.8	28.17	27.73	27.13	25.2	23.36	24.15	23.09	21.52	21.01	20.61	20.31	20.11	19.93
China	3.39	3.47	3.72	4.14	4.37	4.39	4.59	4.96	5.5	6.28	7.39	8.65	9.34	9.98	10.5	11.1	11.68	12.26	12.86
Japan	12.82	13.98	14.49	12.8	11.78	11.31	10.94	10	8.85	7.86	7.97	8.72	8.68	8.36	8.31	8.05	7.87	7.64	7.41
Germany	7.25	6.83	5.87	5.88	6.05	6.49	6.49	6.09	5.89	5.98	5.95	5.73	5.22	5.18	5.03	4.84	4.67	4.48	4.29
India	1.41	1.45	1.48	1.52	1.53	1.58	1.64	1.78	1.84	2.07	2.05	2.19	2.59	2.63	2.73	2.88	3.03	3.17	3.31
Russia	0.9	0.63	0.81	0.96	1.04	1.15	1.4	1.68	2.01	2.33	2.71	2.12	2.35	2.69	2.87	3.02	3.14	3.25	3.37

IMF note of GDP calculation: "Values are based upon GDP in national currency converted to U.S. dollars using market exchange rates (yearly average). Exchange rate projections are provided by country economists for the group of other emerging market and developing countries. Exchanges rates for advanced economies are established in the WEO [World Economic Outlook] assumptions for each WEO exercise. Expenditure–based GDP is total final expenditures at purchasers' prices (including the f.o.b. value of exports of goods and services), less the f.o.b. value of imports of goods and services."

Source: Adapted from data in *World Economic Outlook Database.* International Monetary Fund. September 2011. Accessed 29 October 2011. http://www.imf.org/external/pubs/ft/weo/2011/o2/weodata/index.aspx

* The data for Russia begin in 1992.

43

TABLE 2.3. *Percent of World GDP (Purchasing Power Parity)*, 1980–2016

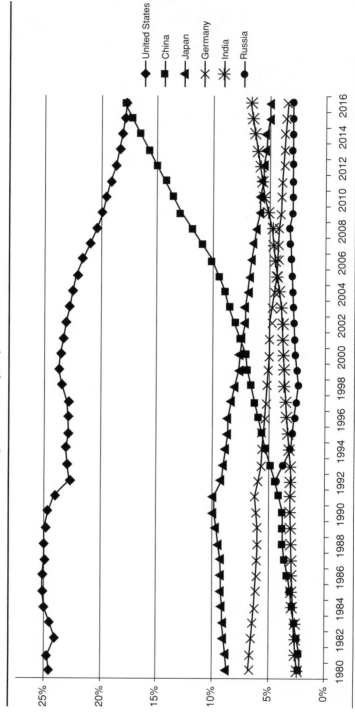

Source: Adapted from data in *World Economic Outlook Database.* International Monetary Fund. September 2011. Accessed 29 October 2011. http://www.imf.org/external/pubs/ft/weo/2011/02/weodata/index.aspx

44

TABLE 2.3 (continued)

	1980	1981	1982	1983	1984	1985	1986	1987	1988	1989	1990	1991	1992	1993	1994	1995	1996	1997
United States	24.64	24.75	24.13	24.57	25.13	25.19	25.22	25.10	25.05	25.01	24.70	24.14	22.76	22.94	23.14	22.89	22.91	22.99
China	2.19	2.26	2.45	2.65	2.91	3.18	3.35	3.60	3.84	3.85	3.88	4.15	4.32	4.83	5.29	5.67	6.01	6.31
Japan	8.65	8.83	9.07	9.11	9.08	9.29	9.25	9.29	9.54	9.69	9.91	10.04	9.23	9.05	8.85	8.71	8.62	8.41
Germany	6.74	6.61	6.52	6.45	6.33	6.22	6.17	6.04	6.00	6.01	6.16	6.34	5.87	5.69	5.66	5.55	5.40	5.28
India	2.53	2.63	2.72	2.82	2.82	2.84	2.89	2.90	3.01	3.10	3.17	3.17	3.02	3.11	3.20	3.31	3.44	3.44
Russia	n/a	n/a	n/a	n/a	n/a	n/a	n/a	n/a	n/a	n/a	n/a	n/a	4.20	3.75	3.18	2.94	2.73	2.66

	1998	1999	2000	2001	2002	2003	2004	2005	2006	2007	2008	2009	2010	2011	2012	2013	2014	2015	2016
United States	23.41	23.70	23.55	23.28	23.06	22.84	22.52	22.26	21.74	21.04	20.43	19.90	19.53	19.11	18.71	18.37	18.10	17.87	17.64
China	6.64	6.90	7.14	7.56	8.02	8.52	8.93	9.46	10.14	11.00	11.74	12.95	13.61	14.35	15.06	15.79	16.51	17.26	18.04
Japan	8.04	7.75	7.61	7.45	7.27	7.12	6.97	6.83	6.63	6.44	6.21	5.87	5.81	5.57	5.49	5.36	5.23	5.06	4.90
Germany	5.24	5.15	5.07	5.04	4.91	4.72	4.56	4.40	4.34	4.27	4.19	4.01	3.96	3.92	3.82	3.71	3.60	3.48	3.37
India	3.56	3.68	3.72	3.78	3.84	3.97	4.10	4.29	4.47	4.67	4.83	5.20	5.46	5.67	5.86	6.07	6.28	6.48	6.69
Russia	2.46	2.53	2.65	2.73	2.78	2.88	2.94	2.99	3.08	3.17	3.25	3.03	3.00	3.01	3.02	3.01	2.99	2.97	2.94

IMF Note: The IMF is not a primary source for purchasing power parity (PPP) data. WEO weights have been created from primary sources and are used solely for purposes of generating country group composites. For primary source information, please refer to one of the following sources: the Organization for Economic Cooperation and Development, the World Bank, or the Penn World Tables.

Source: Adapted from data in World Economic Outlook Database. International Monetary Fund. September 2011. Accessed 29 October 2011. http://www.imf.org/external/pubs/ft/weo/2011/02/weodata/index.aspx.

* The data for Russia begin in 1992.

However, by 2008, the relative share had slipped to 17.7 percent. This change reflected the rapid rise in Chinese production for export, which by 2008 had surged to 17.3 percent of the world total, contrasted with just 7.4 percent a decade earlier.[21] By some estimates, China appears to have become the world's largest manufacturer, a position the United States had held for more than a century, although comparisons remain inexact and do not take into account America's more efficient and productive base and its substantial lead in high-end and high-technology production in such areas as aircraft, electronics, industrial machinery, and scientific and medical equipment.[22]

America's capacity to cope with serious financial pressures at home and competition abroad should be measured not only in terms of economic data. The numbers do matter, but they describe only part of a much broader domestic foundation that encompasses not only economic and military strength, but technology, science, medicine, higher education, culture, demography, the information revolution, and more. Despite periodically expressed concerns, in virtually all these realms the United States continues to rank highly.

As an indication of the breadth and depth of this foundation, in the all-important area of competitiveness the United States consistently ranks among the top countries in the world, with its closest competitors in these rankings being much smaller and far less powerful countries such as Switzerland, Sweden, and Singapore. According to data compiled by the World Economic Forum on the economies of 139 countries, the United States ranked fourth in global competitiveness in 2010–2011, having slipped from first place in 2008–2009 and second place in 2009–2010, a slippage attributable to the effects of

---

[21] The consulting firm IHS Global Insight calculated the U.S. share of world manufacturing in 2009 as 19.9%. In current dollars, it estimated that China would overtake the United States in 2011, while on an inflation-adjusted basis this would occur in 2013–2014. See Peter Marsh, "US Manufacturing Crown Slips," *Financial Times*, June 20, 2010. UNCTAD gives a U.S. figure of 17.7% for 2008, according to data cited in "Balance of Trade and Share of Global Manufacturing," http://www.ourfuture.org/blog-entry/2009104323/balance-trade-and-share-global-manufacturing, accessed July 28, 2010.

[22] *The Economist* estimates that China overtook the United States in 2010. See "Rising Power, Anxious State," Survey, p. 3, June 25, 2011. Also see "China Could Overtake the U.S. as World's Top Manufacturer by 2011," http://www.2point6billion.com/news/2010/06/22/china-could-overtake-u-s-as-worlds-top-manufacturer-by-2011-6113.html, accessed June 29, 2011.

the financial crisis. Among the top ten countries in competitiveness, the only other large economies were those of Germany (in fifth place) and Japan (sixth). China ranked far back, in twenty-seventh place. This particular set of rankings combines a dozen indicators including institutions, infrastructure, macroeconomic stability, higher education, goods and labor market efficiency, financial markets, technology, market size, business sophistication, and innovation.[23] Rankings such as these involve a degree of arbitrariness,[24] but other surveys also rank the United States at or very near the top in competitiveness as well as in categories such as information technology, conditions for companies, and ease of doing business.

Competitiveness also is evident in the performance of American multinational companies. They do not seem to be seriously affected by political considerations that might have diverted business toward firms from countries less identified with the United States. For example, in the commercial realm, despite sporadic calls during the past decade for boycotts of American consumer products, especially in the Middle East and Europe, U.S. brands did not suffer in comparison with their competitors in the same industries. Data for the sales revenues of companies such as Coca-Cola and McDonald's for 2000–2001 and 2003–2004, at the height of the Iraq controversy, showed that American firms did at least as well as their European counterparts.[25] For example, despite their conspicuousness as an American cultural symbol, McDonald's restaurants in France thrived, expanding to more than 1,000 locations.

In higher education, America remains unmatched. According to rankings by China's Shanghai Jiao Tong University, the United States holds seventeen of the top twenty spots among the world's top research universities. (The other three in that top group are Oxford, Cambridge, and Tokyo.) But it not just among the very top universities that the United States excels. In the Shanghai rankings it also occupies

---

[23] World Economic Forum, *Global Competitiveness Report, 2010–2011*, http://www.weforum.org/issues/global-competitiveness, accessed June 28, 2011.

[24] The Geneva-based World Economic Forum bases its ratings on publicly available data for 139 economies and an opinion survey of 13,500 business leaders from those countries.

[25] Peter Katzenstein and Robert Keohane, "Anti-Americanism in World Politics," cited in *The Economist*, December 17, 2005, p. 62.

thirty-five of the top fifty slots and fifty-four of the top one hundred. Here too, there is some arbitrariness in judgment, if not a political thumb on the scale. A 2010 report by the Shanghai Jiao Tong contrived to place four Chinese universities in the top twenty, even though just two years earlier rankings from the same source had shown Chinese institutions well down the list and often being outperformed by other Asian universities.[26] A competing ranking system produced in England by the *Times Higher Education Supplement* accords thirteen of the top twenty slots to U.S. universities, while coincidentally including a generous number of British universities, including four of the top twenty.[27] (See Table 2.4.)

Despite fears that tougher U.S. visa regulations in the aftermath of the 9/11 attacks would discourage applicants from abroad, the number actually has continued to increase, with 586,000 foreign students enrolled for 2009–2010, according to data from the National Science Foundation. This actually represents a 7 percent increase compared with 2001.[28] Despite expansion in the quantity and availability of universities abroad, the relative attractiveness of American institutions remains impressive. It is especially evident for foreign science and engineering students from China, India, and the Middle East. A more important long-term impediment, however, concerns a dysfunctional immigration policy, the result of which is to make it increasingly difficult for well-qualified foreign students who have completed their advanced education in the United States – hitherto a valued and talented addition to American society – to remain in the country in order to pursue their careers.

The breadth and depth of its research universities represents an exceptional asset for the United States, and the quality of higher

---

[26] See "American Universities Maintain Dominance in Latest Shanghai Rankings," *The Chronicle of Higher Education*, August 7, 2008, http://chronicle.com/icons/space.gif, August 7, 2008. And see Shanghai Jiao Tong rankings for 2010, http://www.4icu.org/top200/, accessed July 29, 2010.

[27] Times Higher Education-QS World University Rankings 2009, http://www.timeshighereducation.co.uk/hybrid.asp?typeCode=438, accessed July 29, 2010.

[28] "Foreign-Student Enrollments in U.S. Rise Despite Global Recession," *The Chronicle of Higher Education*, July 8, 2010, http://chronicle.com/article/Foreign-Student-Enrollments-in/66214/, accessed July 29, 2010. Data for 2001 from Peter Schworm, "Foreign Students Flock to the US," *The Boston Globe*, July 5, 2008.

TABLE 2.4. *World University Rankings*

U.S. News and World Report (QS 2009)	Academic Ranking of World Universities 2010 (China, Shanghai Jiao Tong)	QS University Rankings 2010 (UK)
1 Harvard University	Harvard University	University of Cambridge
2 University of Cambridge	University of California, Berkeley	Harvard University
3 Yale University	Stanford University	Yale University
4 University College London	MIT	University College London
5 Imperial College London	University of Cambridge	MIT
6 University of Oxford	Caltech	University of Oxford
7 University of Chicago	Princeton University	Imperial College London
8 Princeton University	Columbia University	University of Chicago
9 MIT	University of Chicago	Caltech
10 Caltech	University of Oxford	Princeton University
11 Columbia University	Yale University	Columbia University
12 University of Pennsylvania	Cornell University	University of Pennsylvania
13 The Johns Hopkins University	University of California, Los Angeles	Stanford University
14 Duke University	University of California, San Diego	Duke University
15 Cornell University	University of Pennsylvania	University of Michigan
16 Stanford University	University of Washington	Cornell University
17 Australia National University	University of Wisconsin, Madison	The Johns Hopkins University
18 McGill University	The Johns Hopkins University/ University of California, San Francisco	ETH Zurich (Swiss Fed. Institute of Technology)
19 University of Michigan	University of Tokyo	McGill University
20 University of Edinburgh/ETH Zurich	University College London	Australia National University

Sources: U.S. News & World Report, World's Best Universities, February 25, 2010, based on QS UK Rankings 2009, http://www.usnews.com/articles/education/worlds-best-universities/2010/02/25/worlds-best-universities-top-400.html, accessed September 12, 2010.

Institute of Higher Education, Shanghai Jiao Tong University, http://www.arwu.org/ARWU2010.jsp, accessed September 12, 2010.

QS World University Rankings 2010, http://www.topuniversities.com/university-rankings/world-university-rankings/2010/results, accessed September 12, 2010.

education in the United States and of the scientific, medical, and high-technology research establishment is also evident in the number and range of active Nobel Prize winners, some 70 percent of whom are employed in the United States. In addition, America benefits from extensive cross-fertilization among universities, governmental and nongovernmental research institutes, and the private sector. The result is to provide the United States with critical mass in many advanced fields, and this edge also serves as a magnet for talented immigrants. The number, density, and spread of research and technology clusters acts as an incubator for new ideas and innovation, and the competitive environment in which they develop attracts start-up capital, skilled personnel, and facilities that convert ideas and inventions into new technologies and products and foster a constant stream of innovation.

Another key factor operating in favor of the United States, and one not always appreciated, is that of population. One advantage comes from sheer size. With 311 million people, the United States is the third most populous country in the world, after China and India, and by far the largest among the most developed countries of the world. Demography also works to the advantage of the United States in terms of the population age profile. While much attention has been focused on the looming retirement of the Baby Boom generation and the consequences for entitlement program costs, it is nonetheless the case that most other large countries are experiencing a more pronounced aging of their populations. For the United States, this shift is occurring to a lesser extent and more slowly than among its competitors. Most European countries and Japan have low birth rates, with total fertility rates (TFR) in the range of 1.3 to 1.8, as compared with a TFR average of 2.1 live births per woman as the rate required to maintain the given size of a population. The TFR of the United States has been close to the 2.1 replacement level – though a slight reduction has been evident during the recession. Live births in 2010 declined by 7 percent from 2007, but including immigration, America continues to experience sustained population growth.[29]

---

[29] U.S. live births in 2010 totaled 4,007,000, compared with 4,317,119 in 2007. During the same period, the birth rate per 1,000 population declined from 14.3 to 12.9. Data from "Births and Deaths: Provisional Data for 2010," National Vital Statistics

Among other major countries, Russia not only exhibits a low TFR of 1.4, but it also has an unusually high death rate for a country at its level of development, so that its overall population has been declining, with three deaths for every two live births in recent years. During the coming decades, China, because of the effects of its one-child policy, will have a larger percentage of its population among the elderly than the United States. Although China's population of 15- to 29-year-olds increased during the previous decade, beginning in 2011, the number of Chinese youth in that age group has begun dropping steeply.[30] Whereas in 1990, only 9 percent of China's population was age sixty or older, compared with 17 percent in the United States, by the year 2050, 32 percent of Chinese will fall into that age group, as against 25 percent in America.[31] Mark Haas argues that as a result of demographic trends of this kind, global aging "will be a potent force for the continuation of US power dominance, both economic and military."[32]

To be sure, the relative predominance and size of the U.S. economy in comparison with other major countries is not the same as a generation ago and it now faces formidable competition from China and other emergent powers. Here too, another historical comparison is worth noting. Britain, even at the height of its international predominance, never had the same margin of relative power and economic weight that the United States has possessed since 1945. A century ago, on the eve of World War I, the United Kingdom had seen its share of world manufacturing fall to around 13 percent of the total and it had already been outpaced by the United States and Germany. By contrast, the United States today remains a far more formidable presence in the world economy. As a result, even with a degree of erosion in the power that the United States possesses relative to other major countries, in

Report, U.S. Centers for Disease Control and Prevention, http://www.cdc.gov/nchs/data/dvs/provisional_tables/Provisional_Table01_2010Dec, accessed June 28, 2011. Previous recessions have seen modest reductions in birth rates.

[30] U.S. Census data, cited in *The Economist*, July 31, 2010. On Russian demographic decline, see Nicholas Eberstadt, "The Dying Bear," *Foreign Affairs*, Vol. 90, No. 6 (November/December 2011): 95–108.

[31] Data from John Plender, "Decline But No Fall," *Financial Times*, November 11, 2009.

[32] Mark L. Haas, "A Geriatric Peace? The Future of U.S. Power in a World of Aging Populations," *International Security*, Vol. 32, No. 1 (Summer 2007): 112–147, at 113.

most dimensions by which power is measured, the margin between America and the others remains substantial.

The Perils of Oil Import Dependence

Another threat to U.S. primacy stems from the extent of its dependence on imported oil and the resultant economic and security vulnerabilities. A generation ago, at the time of the 1973–1974 oil shock, the United States imported 35 percent of its total oil consumption. Over the following three decades, that dependence swelled to more than 60 percent, leaving the country increasingly vulnerable to the impact of events in the Middle East, where some two-thirds of the world's proven supplies of crude oil are located. Although the majority of U.S. oil imports come from North America and sub-Saharan Africa (together, 56 percent), and just 23 percent are supplied from the Middle East and North Africa, this does not insulate America from external events.[33] In the highly integrated world oil system, developments almost anywhere can have an immediate global ripple effect. At times when the international supply/demand balance is tight and there is little spare production capacity, as has periodically been the case, any incident of war, terrorism, political turmoil, or natural disaster can have disproportionate effects on oil prices and availability.

Even in non-crisis circumstances, periods of sustained and widespread economic growth in countries such as China and India can contribute to rapid escalation in world oil prices, as oil demand puts pressure on immediately available supplies. Prior to the softening of the world oil market brought on by financial crisis and recession, rapidly expanding demand had created conditions for extreme volatility. Notably, surging economic growth in Asia, tight supplies elsewhere, and rampant speculation led to a run-up in world oil prices to a high of $147 per barrel in July 2008 before subsiding.

---

[33] Major suppliers of U.S. crude oil and total petroleum imports from North America include Canada 23%, Mexico 11%, and Venezuela 8%; from sub-Saharan Africa: Nigeria 11% and Angola 4%; from the Middle East and North Africa: Saudi Arabia 13%, Iraq 6%, and Algeria 4%. Data from "Crude Oil and Total Petroleum Imports Top 15 Countries," U.S. Energy Information Administration, August 30, 2010, http://www.eia.doe.gov/pub/oil_gas/petroleum/data_publications/company_level_imports/current/import.htm, accessed September 19, 2010.

TABLE 2.5. *Leading World Oil Producers, Million Barrels per Day (mbd)*

Russia	10.3 mbd
Saudi Arabia	10.0
United States	7.5
Iran	4.2
China	4.0
Canada	3.3
Mexico	3.0
United Arab Emirates	2.8
Kuwait	2.5
Venezuela	2.5
Iraq	2.5
Nigeria	2.4
Brazil	2.1
Norway	2.1

Data for countries with annual oil production of 2.0 million barrels per day or above. Includes crude oil, shale oil, oil sands, and natural gas liquids. *Source: BP Statistical Review of World Energy, June* 2011, http://www.bp.com/liveassets/bp_internet/globalbp/globalbp_uk_english/reports_and_publications/statistical_energy_review_2011/STAGING/local_assets/pdf/oil_section_2011.pdf. Accessed October 26, 2011.

Subsequently, events of the Arab Spring of 2011, including upheavals in the oil-producing countries of Libya and Yemen, helped push world oil prices once again above the $100-per-barrel level.[34] Experiences such as these provide evidence that a future crisis affecting oil supplies, especially in the Persian Gulf region, could have serious domestic consequences. In addition, enormous oil revenues also strengthen the hands of producing countries with regimes that have interests quite divergent from those of the United States or that are politically hostile. Examples of such regimes include Iran, Venezuela, Libya, Russia, and others in the Middle East and the Persian Gulf.

---

[34] Crude oil pricing is commonly cited either as West Texas Intermediate (WTI) Crude, traded on the New York Mercantile Exchange (NYMEX), or as Brent (North Sea) traded in London. E.g., in late December 2011, the spot price for crude oil traded on NYMEX was priced at $98 per barrel, while Brent was at $108.

The core problem is one of vulnerability rather than oil or energy import dependence per se. Since the first oil shock in 1973, the proclamation that we must "end our dependence on foreign oil" has been a hardy perennial of politicians and presidents from Richard Nixon to Barack Obama.[35] But completely ending oil imports is both infeasible and unnecessary. It is infeasible because the prodigious quantity of oil imports – some 10 million barrels per day (mbd) out of a total domestic consumption of 18 mbd – cannot at any time in the foreseeable future be entirely replaced through domestic production, conservation, or fuel substitution. And it is unnecessary because the real need is to significantly lessen rather than end the high levels of dependence. To achieve this requires a robust and diverse mix of energy sources and measures so that no one event or crisis in itself can threaten America's economic well-being or national security.

The critical need is to reduce America's vulnerability to the vagaries of supply and demand so that it is not exposed to damaging run-ups in price, or the risk of supply interruptions, or energy blackmail in the event of a grave crisis in the Persian Gulf region. The quest for an effective energy policy has seen numerous proposed solutions, many of them impractical, inefficient, or irrelevant – if not all three. These have included, for example, synthetic fuels, hydrogen-fueled vehicles, corn-based ethanol, nuclear fusion, and clean coal. The practical solutions are more prosaic, far more effective, and – absent a dire crisis – politically difficult. These solutions require addressing both the consumption *and* supply sides of the energy balance – measures whose proponents often can be found in a state of political conflict with one another. Such measures include efforts on the consumption side to improve energy efficiency and conservation, and on the production side to increase the production of energy, especially natural gas and oil, along with newer technologies including wind and solar when and where these can be cost efficient.

More than two-thirds of the petroleum used in America is consumed in the transportation sector; hence a key task is to take the steps

---

[35] For example, Oval Office address by President Barack Obama, "We must...end our dependence on foreign oil." In "Remarks by the President in Address to the Nation on the End of Combat Operations in Iraq," Office of the Press Secretary, August 31, 2010, whitehouse.gov, accessed September 1, 2010.

necessary for much more efficient fuel use as well as continuing to develop domestic and foreign supplies. The political obstacles here have been familiar and daunting. Both regulation and market signals are essential in order to encourage more fuel-efficient cars and trucks. Modest steps were put in place with the 1975 adoption by Congress of the "CAFE" standards (Corporate Average Fuel Efficiency) mandating gradual adoption of a 27.5 miles-per-gallon (mpg) average for cars. These were adopted over the bitter opposition of the domestic auto industry and its unions.

Further improvements in fuel efficiency requirements were long delayed, but in recent years the tightening of standards has faced less of an obstacle from this now weaker industry and its unions. That plus the effects of steep increases in world oil prices, worries about future oil supplies, Middle East instability, the economic crisis, and environmental concerns led to a 2009 agreement to require cars and light trucks to reach a 31.4 mpg average by 2016. In turn, that agreement was followed by a July 2011 accord setting a standard of 54.5 mpg by 2025. Though seemingly technical, these agreements are quite important and will have an enduring impact on oil consumption. The achievement demonstrates that in this realm – as in others – although necessary measures could have been taken earlier, the importance and urgency of the task finally led to results.

Another far-reaching measure would be to structure incentives and disincentives for individuals and businesses through the use of higher gasoline taxes. These are common in Europe and large parts of Asia, though politically anathema to most elected politicians and much of the public. The virtue of higher fuel taxes is that these increase the incentives for efficient use of gasoline and help reduce oil consumption and imports. In turn, this would lower the balance-of-trade deficit (44 percent of which is from oil), thus lessening the vast revenues now flowing from the United States to foreign oil producers.

If taking steps to markedly reduce gasoline consumption has faced serious obstacles, much the same is true of efforts to increase energy and electricity production. Opposition, often quite passionate, comes from staunch environmental advocates. It also is a product of the NIMBY (not-in-my-back-yard) syndrome. A case in point has been the proposed wind farm in Nantucket Sound, five miles off the coast of Cape Cod and opposed for many years by local residents including the Kennedy family. In recent decades, obstacles to drilling for oil in the Arctic Natural Wildlife Refuge (ANWR) and to coastal and deepwater drilling off America's coasts have put huge areas off limits – though the catastrophic 2010 BP-Deepwater Horizon oil spill in the Gulf of Mexico provides a graphic reminder that virtually all sources of energy production and transport involve real risk.

Discoveries of vast quantities of deep natural gas, known as unconventional gas, or shale gas, have the potential to provide major benefits. Until the middle of the past decade, it was widely assumed that the country would soon see long-term shortages of natural gas. Yet as a result of advances in technology, including computing, the ability to map subsurface resources, and hydraulic fracturing, or "fracking" (the use of deep and horizontal drilling plus the high-pressure injection of water, sand and chemicals to release gas from the surrounding rock), America now has the prospect of ample supplies for a century or more. An added benefit here is that rather than having to import large quantities of liquefied natural gas (LNG) from Qatar, Russia, Libya, Nigeria, and even Iran, the United States is likely to become an exporter of it. Not only will this have a favorable bearing on America's own energy security and energy revenues; it also helps create a surplus of natural gas abroad, which can lessen the potential economic and political influence of supplier countries.

Natural gas now provides approximately one-fourth of America's total energy consumption. For electricity generation, where its share has been rising rapidly, it is mainly an alternative to coal and it produces significantly lower emissions of particulates and greenhouse gasses. Gas is also a major source for residential and commercial heating and for industrial use. In addition, natural gas has the potential to power busses and trucks. Though not yet available as an option in the United States, natural gas can also be converted into methanol as a liquid fuel, as is the case in Brazil.

In addition to a dramatic rise in natural gas, America is now on the cusp of a major increase in domestic oil production. The same fracking technique has the potential to release significant quantities of "tight oil" from deep underground shale rock formations. In addition to improved technologies for extracting oil from offshore deposits in the Gulf of Mexico and in older, depleted oil fields, this technique has played a major role in reversing a long decline in U.S. oil production.

Oil output is already booming in North Dakota and in parts of Texas, and in 2009, domestic oil production actually rose for the first time since 1971. Together with modest reductions in domestic oil consumption, changes in the energy balance are becoming evident, so that the proportion of domestic demand met by net oil imports has dropped from more than 60 percent in 2005 to 47 percent in 2010. Moreover, leading energy experts are optimistic about the potential, suggesting that within a decade, oil imports might even be reduced from 10 mbd to as low as 3 mbd.[36] To be sure, these changes, especially in the exploitation of tight oil, represent a highly promising potential more than a fully accomplished achievement, and the ability to scale up from initial projects will be an important determinant. Of equal or greater importance will be environmental policy, onshore and offshore drilling permits, pipeline locations, and regulatory decisions.

Opinion polls indicate that the American public sees the need to develop more domestic oil and gas resources, and a survey of likely voters found 75 percent saying that the United States was not doing enough in this regard.[37] Yet these same results also show underlying political differences on whether to emphasize increasing supply or reducing demand. Thus 59 percent of Democrats favor reducing oil demand over increasing the supply, while 69 percent of Republicans prefer increasing the supply. In reality, both the supply and demand sides of the energy balance require attention and exclusive emphasis on one or the other will not provide an effective response.

Energy, economics, and security form a complex mosaic. Over the years, growing dependence on imported oil has created a serious vulnerability, in which events taking place half a world away can trigger steep price increases or supply disruptions. However, for the first time in a generation, the practical possibility of making significant inroads

---

[36] Ed Crooks, "Pendulum Swings on American Oil Dependence," *Financial Times*, October 31, 2011. The estimate of possible reduction in oil imports to 3 mbd by the early 2020s is from Edward Morse, head of commodities research at Citigroup. Also see Reuters, "Unconventional Oil Shifting the Energy Balance of Power," *ArabNews.com*, November 22, 2011, http://arabnews.com/economy/article536856. ece?service=print, accessed November 25, 2011.

[37] "75% Say U.S. Not Doing Enough to Develop Its Gas and Oil Resources," *Rasmussen Reports*, June 29, 2011, http://www.rasmussenreports.com/public_content/politics/current_events/environment_energy/75_say_u_s_not_doing_enough_to_develop_its_gas_and_oil_resources, accessed June 29, 2011.

in oil import dependence is at hand. Now, an effective energy policy is much more a matter of political and policy choice than of overcoming resource or technology limitations.

Power and Domestic Capacity

When all is said and done, does the United States possess the material attributes, economic strength, and human resources to maintain a leading international role comparable to the one it has played since the end of World War II? The importance of this role should not be underestimated. It affects not only the national interest and security of the United States itself, but the stability of the global order that the United States has underwritten during the past seven decades.

The human potential, flexibility, openness, entrepreneurial skills, and scientific, educational, and technical assets within the United States are available to underpin this role, as they have been in the past. The underlying question is less one of capacity and potential than of policy, persistence, and political will. The answer is more likely to be found in domestic attitudes and institutions than in any straightforward calculation of annual GDP figures, or projections of whether and when the size of the Chinese economy will surpass that of the United States. It is to that fundamental question that the next chapter turns.

3

American Attitudes and Institutions

"The great privilege of the Americans does not consist in being more enlightened than any other nations, but in being able to repair the faults they may commit."

– Alexis de Tocqueville[1]

Can America sustain an international role comparable to the one it has played in world affairs for the past seven decades, that is, from the early years of World War II to the present time? The answer depends both on the domestic basis on which this leadership rests and on the international setting in which it takes place. This chapter delves into the attitudes, policies, and institutions that shape this special role and determine America's ability to lead.

As Tocqueville's words written in the 1830s suggest, informed observers have long noted America's capacity to adapt, repair, and constantly renew itself. But if there is an enduring basis for the robustness and resilience of the United States as an economy, society, and polity, there remain other attributes that can impede successful adaptation to new challenges and threats. The unique characteristics of America, embodied in exceptionalism and the openness of its society, have made it a leader in world affairs and a magnet for people from other lands. The costs of exceptionalism can be found, however, in

---

[1] *Democracy in America*, the Henry Reeve text, rev. by Francis Bowen and edited by Phillips Bradley (New York: Vintage, 1945), p. 239.

the often raucous political climate, the unwieldiness of some of the institutions bequeathed by the Founding Fathers, and the difficulty of crafting solutions for pressing problems until these reach crisis propor- tions. Political polarization and domestic dissensus exacerbate these tendencies and have been increasingly evident among political elites since at least the early 1990s. As a result, partisan rancor and inability to agree on national policies and strategies could prove to be greater impediments to America's staying power than the more commonly cited problems of economic difficulty and military overstretch.

Public Attitudes

Throughout World War II and much of the Cold War, international affairs ranked high on the list of public concerns. The threat to America's national interest and way of life posed first by Nazi Germany and Imperial Japan, and soon afterward by the Soviet Union, drew the attention and concern of American voters and provided a basis of pub- lic support for the human and material costs of what became a super- power role. Global competition with America's adversaries included hot and cold wars. Conscription, which remained in effect until 1973, meant that most able-bodied males faced the likelihood, even if not the certainty, of military service. High defense budgets were common, amounting to between 10 and 14 percent of GDP during the 1950s, 7 to 9 percent in the 1960s, and 5 to 7 percent during most of the 1970s and 1980s.[2] These expenditures and others sustained an enor- mous military establishment, with bases, armed forces, and alliances reaching across the globe, and backed by a large intelligence establish- ment. During these years, the United States maintained an expansive foreign aid program, first with the Marshall Plan and later the Agency for International Development, as well as an ambitious program of international broadcasting and public diplomacy (Voice of America, Radio Free Europe, and the United States Information Agency).

With the opening of the Berlin Wall in 1989, the end of the Cold War, and then the breakup of the Soviet Union, foreign policy no

---

[2] Data from "Table 3.1: Outlays by Superfunction and Function: 1940–2009," in *Office of Management and Budget, Historical Tables, Budget of the United States Govern- ment, Fiscal Year 2005* (Washington, DC: 2004), pp. 45–52.

longer ranked high on the list of concerns on voters' minds. The 1991 Gulf War provided a temporary exception to this pattern, but by the time of the 1992 presidential election, only 9 percent of voters cited foreign policy as one of the top two issues influencing their vote.[3] Conflicts in the Balkans during the mid- and late 1990s and sporadic terrorist bombings aimed at American targets in Saudi Arabia, Yemen, Kenya, and Tanzania attracted brief attention, but not until the 9/11 terrorist attacks did foreign and national security policy reemerge as leading subjects of public concern. Public interest then remained high in response to the wars in Afghanistan and Iraq.

With the financial crisis in 2008, the election of Barack Obama as president, and a sluggish economic recovery, public attention to foreign policy again declined. By the time of the November 2010 midterm elections, the percentage of Americans citing war, national security, or terrorism as the nation's single most important problem had dropped into the low single digits. A mere 3 percent listed the fear of war, and no more than 1 percent cited national security, war in Iraq, or terrorism. By contrast, economic and to some extent leadership concerns were overwhelmingly dominant: 33 percent cited the economy in general, 28 percent unemployment, 11 percent dissatisfaction with government, Congress, or politicians, 7 percent the federal budget deficit or national debt, and 6 percent poor leadership.[4] A slow economic recovery, stubbornly high unemployment, and broad and deep concern about extraordinary levels of national debt and deficit led to widespread voter discontent and large Republican gains in the November 2010 elections. These events, along with increasingly skeptical attitudes toward the role of government and the costs of foreign commitments among large sectors of the electorate, could signal reduced public willingness to pay the price of international leadership.

Public optimism about the role of government has been a casualty, but here too a sense of proportion is required in interpreting the results of opinion polls. On the one hand, by the autumn of 2010, public

---

3 Voter Research and Surveys. Election Day poll conducted November 3, 1992, by a consortium of CBS, ABC, NBC, and CNN. An August 1995 poll found only 4% who described foreign policy as the biggest problem facing the country. *The New York Times*/CBS News poll, cited in *The New York Times*, October 1, 1995.

4 "Most Important Problem," *Gallup.com*, October 29, 2010, http://www.gallup.com/poll/1675/Most-Important-Problem.aspx, accessed October 29, 2010.

optimism on the working of "our system of government" had dropped to a thirty-six-year low, with 33 percent of respondents describing themselves as optimistic, 20 percent pessimistic, and the remainder uncertain or without an opinion. However, when probed for their reasons, Americans replied, by a 3-to-1 margin, that the problem is the people running the government, not the government itself.[5]

Another indicator of social cohesion concerns confidence in national institutions. Here the results are mixed. Americans express relatively high esteem for the military, small business, the police, organized religion, and the Supreme Court, with 77 percent or more indicating "some" or "quite a lot" of confidence. They give lower marks, however, to the banks, organized labor, big business, health maintenance organizations, and Congress.[6]

For the most part, the available data do not indicate public demand for serious retrenchment in foreign and military policy. It is true that Americans have come to favor a withdrawal of U.S. troops from Afghanistan as soon as possible. Even so, it was only after nearly ten years of war there that a majority (56 percent) expressed this view.[7] In contrast, an authoritative national survey of public opinion on foreign policy, conducted by the Chicago Council on Global Affairs, showed substantial, even surprising, continuity.[8] Despite two-thirds of respondents agreeing that reducing the federal deficit is "very important," the public continues to express support for international engagement. Two-thirds of Americans think it important for the United States to

---

[5] "Public Optimism Hits a 36-year Low in Views of the 'System of Government,'" ABC News/Yahoo News Poll, October 26, 2010, http://abcnews.go.com/Site/page?id= 11965387, accessed October 27, 2010.

[6] Jeffrey M. Jones, "Americans Most Confident in Military, Least in Congress: Confidence in most institutions below their historical averages," *Gallup.com*, http://www .gallup.com/poll/148163/Americans-Confident-Military-Least-Congress.aspx?utm_ source=alert&utm_medium=email&utm_campaign=syndication&utm_content= morelink&utm_term=The%20Presidency, accessed July 1, 2011.

[7] Sara Sorcher, "Poll: Americans Who Favor Withdrawing Troops Quickly at All-Time High," *National Journal*, June 21, 2011, http://nationaljournal.com/nationalsecurity/ poll-americans-who-favor-withdrawing-troops-quickly-at-all-time-high-20110621, accessed July 6, 2011.

[8] Chicago Council on Global Affairs, *Constrained Internationalism: Adapting to New Realities: Results of a 2010 National Survey of Public Opinion* (Chicago: September 2010). The survey has been conducted every four years from 1974 to 2002 and biennially since 2002.

take an active part in world affairs, and more than eight in ten believe it is "very" or "somewhat" desirable to exert strong leadership. A majority even believe maintaining superior power worldwide is a "very important" foreign policy goal.[9] Support for engagement is somewhat selective, in that respondents approve multilateral action via the UN and – as was the case in Libya – prefer to remain on the sidelines for conflicts not seen as threatening to the United States. Nonetheless, the public continues to indicate strong support for the military as well as for the use of force against terrorism and nuclear proliferation. A majority also favor long-term retention of military bases.[10]

On balance, this level of support for foreign engagement is remarkable at a time of severe economic stringency and in which voters have reacted at the ballot box by ousting numerous incumbents. One underlying explanation may be attributable to American exceptionalism and deep-seated attitudes about the legitimacy of the use of force. Data here comes from a large-scale survey of public opinion in twelve European countries and the United States conducted annually by the German Marshall Fund. To the question of whether war is necessary to obtain justice under some circumstances, 76 percent of Americans answer yes, but only 28 percent of European Union respondents agree. Responses to this question have remained consistent over the past several years, and among the European countries polled, only in Britain did a majority (61 percent) concur with the statement. The transatlantic divide is even greater among those who strongly agree about the use of force (49 percent in the United States versus 8 percent in the EU).[11]

Opinion polls indicate that the broader public remains less polarized than policy elites and may thus be more receptive to pragmatic solutions for pressing problems. In addition, other public attitudes make it unlikely that American society will favor any large-scale repudiation of foreign commitments. For example, surveys by major polling organizations have repeatedly asked people how proud they are to be Americans and found consistently favorable responses. In January 2001, a

[9] Ibid., p. 4.

[10] Ibid., pp. 5–6.

[11] *Transatlantic Trends: Leaders, Key Findings 2011* (Washington, DC: German Marshall Fund of the United States, 2011), p. 10. Also see *Transatlantic Trends, Key Findings 2010*, p. 18. Surveys conducted June-July 2010. Additional data at: http://www.transatlantictrends.org

Gallup poll found 87 percent saying they were either extremely proud or very proud. A decade later, 75 percent called the United States "the greatest country in the world," and partisan differences in responses to this question were negligible, with 75 percent of Democrats and 80 percent of Republicans giving a positive answer.[12] More recent polls continue to indicate a strong sense of belief in America. A CBS poll taken in May 2011, shortly after the successful operation to kill Osama bin Laden, found 86 percent describing themselves as very proud or extremely proud to be Americans; and a Fox News poll conducted just before the Fourth of July 2011 found 69 percent of voters proud of the country, even though a similar number thought the Founding Fathers would not be proud if they were alive now.[13]

Other indications of public attitudes include tolerance for military casualties, continuing success in recruitment and performance of the volunteer military, and the ongoing high quality of the armed services officer corps. Together with the persistence of lethal foreign threats, especially from terrorism and nuclear proliferation, these responses suggest that a sufficient degree of domestic cohesion and foreign policy consensus is likely to persist within American society.

Domestic Doctrine and Policy

Dramatic differences of style and sometimes substance have often characterized the foreign policies of successive American presidents. Even so, the record of the past seven decades embodies important elements of continuity, and these can be found even in the successive Clinton, Bush, and Obama administrations, covering most of the post–Cold War and post-9/11 periods. These presidents and their predecessors explicitly acknowledged the unique role of the United States in maintaining international security and a stable global order.

---

[12] Earlier polls cited in the ABC News report were conducted by Gallup, *USA Today*, and Roper. http://abcnews.go.com/Site/page?id=11965387, accessed October 27, 2010.

[13] The CBS Poll is cited in Karlyn Bowman, "Polls on Patriotism and Military Service," *AEI Studies in Public Opinion*, June 28, 2011, http://www.aei.org/paper/100231. For the Fox News Poll, see Dana Blanton, "Americans Proud of U.S., but Don't Think Founders Would Be Today," Fox News Poll, July 01, 2011, http://www.foxnews.com/us/2011/07/01/fox-news-poll-americans-proud-us-but-dont-think-founders-would-be-today/#ixzz1RMHxWi8m, accessed July 6, 2011.

In the case of the Obama administration, whose tenacity and commitment to international leadership ("leading from behind" in the words of an Obama advisor) has been called into question by critics, a case can be made that the president values the unique role the United States has played.[14] This was evident in his December 2009 speech accepting the Nobel Peace Prize:

> Yet the world must remember that it was not simply international institutions – not just treaties and declarations – that brought stability to a post–World War II world. Whatever mistakes we have made, the plain fact is this: the United States of America has helped underwrite global security for more than six decades with the blood of our citizens and the strength of our arms.... We have borne this burden not because we seek to impose our will. We have done so out of enlightened self-interest – because we seek a better future for our children and grandchildren, and we believe that their lives will be better if other peoples' children and grandchildren can live in freedom and prosperity.

The Obama administration in practice displayed conflicting impulses. Despite campaign rhetoric, the president did not seek immediate withdrawal from Iraq, although he continued a steady drawdown of troops and increasingly disengaged from efforts to shape Iraq's future, putting at risk the hard-fought accomplishments of seven years of war. In Afghanistan, he committed 33,000 additional troops for a "surge" and deployed an accomplished commander (General David Petraeus) with a mission to prevail in counterinsurgency. However, he also began the process of troop withdrawal just one year after the full complement of American and coalition troops had been deployed, with the aim of removing the surge troops prior to the 2012 presidential election, thereby signaling to all sides in the region an uncertain level of determination and purpose. For al-Qaeda and the Taliban, the implication was that it was best to bide their time. For others, it cautioned them to be wary about identifying with an American patron whose irresolution was to be feared, despite a decade of commitment measured in money, material, and blood.

Elsewhere too there was ambivalence about the uses of American power. On the one hand, there were indications of leadership and authority, with reassurances to East Asian countries anxious about an

---

[14] An Obama advisor described the President's Libya policy as "leading from behind." Quoted in Ryan Lizza, "The Consequentialist," *The New Yorker*, May 2, 2011.

increasingly truculent China and extensive use of lethal drone attacks against insurgents in the rugged terrain along the Afghanistan-Pakistan border, as well as in Yemen and Somalia. The administration also expanded economic and trade sanctions aimed at Iran's nuclear program. On the other hand, there were continued ambiguities, as in repeated but mostly fruitless outreach to adversaries, a de-emphasis of relations with allies, and a determination to pursue a "reset" in relations with Russia, despite limited results. These efforts included repeated overtures to the regime in Teheran and a subdued response to brutal repression there. Despite Syrian President Bashar al-Assad's massive killing of peaceful protesters, his alignment with Iran, Hezbollah, and Hamas, and Syria's disruptive role in Iraq and Lebanon, there was reluctance to call for his ouster. Only after half a year had passed and the civilian death toll in Syria had mounted into the thousands did the administration issue a statement. Even then, the initial demand was not made publicly by the president himself, in contrast to the way in which he had called for Egyptian president Hosni Mubarak to leave office. Above all, there was a palpable sense that economic and financial constraints imposed new limits on America's capacity to act. This was especially evident on the part of a president who had been photographed displaying a copy of Fareed Zakaria's declinist work, *The Post-American World.*

For its part, the previous administration of George W. Bush had also been characterized as departing from the main tenets of previous national security policy – albeit in the opposite direction. The Bush administration was widely criticized for acting without the restraint previously imposed by bipolarity during the Cold War years, or it was said to have abandoned multilateral practice in order to act unilaterally. But such accounts do not accurately describe American doctrine and practice. As John Lewis Gaddis and others have noted, the United States has historically reacted to being attacked by adopting strategies of primacy and preemption. Its neighbors in the eighteenth and nineteenth centuries found the United States a "dangerous nation."[15] And since World War II, presidents of both parties have described America's international role in ways that go well beyond the kind of limited

---

[15] See John Lewis Gaddis, *Surprise, Security, and the American Experience* (Cambridge, MA: Harvard University Press, 2004), and Robert Kagan, *Dangerous Nation* (New York: Knopf, 2006).

engagement that some critics insist is a more consistent or desirable strategy.

President Harry Truman, for example, in his March 1947 speech to a joint session of Congress setting out what came to be known as the Truman doctrine, asserted that "it must be the policy of the United States to support free peoples who are resisting attempted subjugation by armed minorities or by outside pressures." John Kennedy's 1961 inaugural address proclaimed that "we shall pay any price, bear any burden, meet any hardship, support any friend, and oppose any foe, in order to assure the survival and the success of liberty."

Ronald Reagan's State of the Union address in February 1985 insisted: "We must not break faith with those who are risking their lives – on every continent from Afghanistan to Nicaragua – to defy Soviet aggression and secure rights which have been ours from birth. Support for freedom fighters is self-defense."

Bill Clinton's 1993 inaugural address asserted: "Our hopes, our hearts, our hands, are with those on every continent who are building democracy and freedom. Their cause is America's cause." In July 1994, Clinton's National Security Strategy of Engagement and Enlargement advocated expanding the community of democracies and market economies. And in his January 1997 second inaugural address, Clinton stated: "America stands alone as the world's indispensable nation."

In view of these precedents, the Bush administration's embrace of both democratization and primacy, as evidenced in its 2002 National Security Strategy and in Bush's second inaugural address of January 2005, was consistent with past rhetorical statements of American doctrine. In the latter speech, Bush proclaimed: "[I]t is the policy of the United States to seek and support the growth of democratic movements and institutions in every nation and culture, with the ultimate goal of ending tyranny in our world." This, though, was not the unrestrained crusade sometimes attributed to him. Bush made clear that "This is not primarily the task of arms.... America will not impose our own style of government on the unwilling.... Our goal instead is to help others find their own voice, attain their own freedom, and make their own way." He also acknowledged that the "great objective of ending tyranny" is a long-term task, "the concentrated work of generations."

It is also commonplace to assert that before 9/11, American foreign policy had been multilateral in character, in that Democratic and Republican administrations built on international institutions, embraced alliances, and deliberately accepted a kind of "self-binding" to international agreements, institutions, and regimes to secure common objectives.[16] But the record of the past six decades is far more varied than implied by the frequently described contrast between a multilateral past and a unilateral Bush era. Harry Truman sent American forces to Korea in 1950 without waiting for UN authorization, President Dwight Eisenhower ordered U.S. troops to Lebanon in 1958, and John F. Kennedy appeared ready to launch a preemptive attack on Soviet missiles in Cuba had the Russians not backed down during the October 1962 missile crisis. In addition, Presidents Kennedy, Johnson, Nixon, and Ford dispatched American troops to Indochina, Ronald Reagan invaded Grenada, and George H. W. Bush intervened in Panama. The elder Bush also worked closely with Chancellor Helmut Kohl to achieve German unification, despite the reservations of Britain, France, and the Soviet Union, and President Clinton used Tomahawk missiles and combat aircraft to strike targets in Sudan, Afghanistan, and Iraq. In addition, Clinton launched the 1999 air war in Kosovo with NATO agreement but without formal approval by the UN Security Council.

Other evidence of policy continuity between the Republican administration of George H. W. Bush and that of the Democrat Bill Clinton can be found in the more or less bipartisan character of decisions to intervene with military force between 1989 and 2001. Ivo Daalder and Robert Kagan observed that out of eight such interventions during those years, four were carried out under Democratic presidents and four by Republicans. They noted that the circumstances in which a president may need to use force have increased since 9/11, as these now include terrorism, weapons proliferation, and prevention of genocide, as well as in response to traditional forms of aggression.[17]

---

[16] John Ikenberry, *After Victory: Institutions, Strategic Restraint and the Rebuilding of Order After Major Wars* (Princeton, NJ: Princeton University Press, 2001); and "The End of the Neoconservative Movement," *Survival*, Vol. 46, No. 1 (Spring 2004): 7–22.

[17] The authors also advocated efforts among democratic states as a way of securing domestic consensus for the use of force. See Ivo Daalder and Robert Kagan, "The Next Intervention," *The Washington Post*, August 6, 2007; also "America and the Use of Force: Sources of Legitimacy" (Muscatine, IA: The Stanley Foundation, June 2007).

Domestic Capacity

Can the United States sustain the costs of its global role and its national security policy? The difficulty of the task has increased substantially since the financial crisis that erupted in September 2008, and the answers are not simple. Viewed historically, the burden of defense spending, as a percentage of GDP, seems manageable. Including expenditures on the Iraq and Afghan wars, America currently devotes 4.9 percent of its GDP to defense. This contrasts with figures of 6.2 percent at the height of the Reagan buildup in the mid-1980s and up to 10 percent and more during the Truman, Eisenhower, and Kennedy years. Indeed, at the time of Eisenhower's inauguration in January 1953, and with the Korean War still ongoing, defense expenditures accounted for 13 percent of GDP.

There are, however, important differences that make sustaining these costs more difficult than might seem to be the case from the existing GDP percentages alone. Whether or not the troop drawdown in Iraq is completed and commitments in Afghanistan are reduced or even ended altogether, the baseline defense budget, without the cost of two wars, amounts to 3.5 percent of GDP. However, the price tag for replacing worn-out, depleted, and obsolete equipment for the army, air force, navy, and marines will be enormous, and expensive new weapon systems remain to be funded. For example, the average age of some of the bomber fleet and of tanker aircraft, essential for refueling planes on many combat, transport, and support missions, is close to fifty years.[18] In addition, the costs of new ships and aircraft have soared, so that it becomes much more difficult to replace old equipment on a one-for-one basis. Thus the number of ships the U.S. Navy is able to purchase each year has declined since the 1980s from seventeen to six.[19]

Meanwhile, the pending retirement of the Baby Boom generation, looming deficits in the Social Security, Medicare, and Medicaid budgets, and a gradually aging population pose increasing claims on national resources. The resource problems are made still more acute by the intense partisan rancor that has increasingly characterized

[18] Richard B. Andres, "Up in the Air," *American Interest* (September/October 2010): 32.
[19] Seth Cropsey, "Ebb Tide," *American Interest* (September/October 2010): 19.

American politics. At least since the late 1990s, with the Clinton impeachment scandals, and arguably since 1994, when the Republicans under Newt Gingrich and their Contract for America gained control of the House of Representatives for the first time in forty years, the climate among political elites has become more polarized than during the Vietnam era. This acrimony intensified with the contested outcome of the 2000 presidential election, the war in Iraq, and a heated 2008 presidential election contest. Then, with the coming to office of Barack Obama, there were sharp and even angry debates about his policies and controversial legislation passed by the Democratic majorities in Congress in 2009–2010, especially the fiscal stimulus, health care, and financial regulation. Though data from opinion polling indicates that the public at large is significantly less polarized than are political elites and members of Congress, these events and the contentious political climate accompanying them have made it difficult to achieve bipartisan consensus on high-stakes issues. As noted in Chapter 1, political polarization in Congress is now more pronounced than at any time since 1879 and the end of the post–Civil War reconstruction era.[20]

Even so, a degree of historical perspective is valuable in viewing the acrimonious rhetoric and ad hominem attacks that mark contemporary political discourse. It is thus useful to recall that among the Founding Fathers, political debate was often vitriolic and sometimes quite brutal. Critics questioned George Washington's patriotism, and, as adversaries at the end of the eighteenth century, Hamiltonians and Jeffersonians depicted each other in conspiratorial terms. In the presidential election of 1800, Federalist newspapers wrote that with Thomas Jefferson as president, "murder, robbery, rape, adultery, and incest will be openly taught and practiced, the air will be rent with the cries of the distressed, the soil will be soaked with blood, and the nation black with crimes."[21] In 1828, the death of Andrew Jackson's wife, Rachel, shortly after his election as president, was said to have

---

[20] Nolan McCarty, Keith T. Poole, and Howard Rosenthal, *Polarized America: The Dance of Ideology and Unequal Riches* (Cambridge, MA: MIT Press, 2006), and "Party Polarization: 1879–2009," updated 4 January 2010, http://polarizedamerica .com/#POLITICALPOLARIZATION, accessed June 30, 2010.

[21] *Connecticut Courant*, September 20, 1800, quoted in James R. Sharpe, *American Politics in the Early Republic: The New Nation in Crisis* (New Haven, CT: Yale University Press, 1993), p. 227.

been precipitated by shock at scurrilous press attacks in which, over a technicality concerning the divorce from her first husband, she was depicted as a bigamist and a whore. Nor should we forget how bitter the national divide over slavery became, ultimately erupting in the Civil War and the death of 660,000 soldiers on American soil.

These examples from past centuries should serve as a reminder about overstating contemporary divides. A massive and authoritative study by Robert Putnam and David Campbell identifies a deep polarization in American political and religious life, as well as in the overall culture. In addition, although much attention has been focused on the Christian right for exacerbating cultural divisions, this survey finds liberal congregations to be the most politicized. Nonetheless, Putnam and Campbell's major conclusion is that the society has become far more accepting of diversity, and – unlike polarization prior to the Civil War – this tolerance, especially among younger Americans, will keep these fissures from tearing the country apart.[22]

To be sure, some have argued that domestic polarization along with bitter disagreements about Iraq and the war on terror have eroded America's ability to sustain its international role, and they argue for a scaling back of foreign commitments in order to stabilize the political foundations for foreign policy.[23] While overextension is to be avoided, it is not evident that reduced overseas commitments and a less engaged foreign policy are really what matter most. Political dissensus and public judgments about whether foreign interventions will succeed or fail ultimately are of greater consequence than the scale of intervention itself. Domestic support is a sine qua non for sustainable foreign policy commitments, and there is a tendency to assume that public reluctance to bear the costs of foreign interventions is a function of increasing casualties.[24] However, Christopher Gelpi, Peter Feaver, and Jason Reifler have shown that public tolerance for the human toll of war is mainly affected by beliefs about the likelihood of success and

---

[22] Robert D. Putnam and David E. Campbell, *American Grace: How Religion Divides and Unites Us* (New York: Simon & Schuster, 2010).

[23] For example, Charles Kupchan and Peter Trubowitz, "Grand Strategy for a Divided America," *Foreign Affairs*, Vol. 86, No. 4 (July/August 2007): 71–83.

[24] Especially the work of John E. Mueller, who argued that declining support for war was directly related to increasing casualties. See *War, Presidents, and Public Opinion* (New York: Wiley, 1973).

the rightness or wrongness of the war. In their analysis, expectations about success are what matters most.[25]

The problems of maintaining the domestic basis for America's world role are not merely those of affordability or of maintaining public support. Aaron Friedberg emphasizes the long-term challenge of bringing means and ends into alignment. He observes that this will be a daunting task, especially in view of the fact that since the early 1960s, the government has been without a mechanism for sustained interagency planning and for bringing the conflicting demands of finance and strategy into some kind of long-term balance.[26] These organizational tasks often get less attention, but they are no less an obstacle to effective conduct of foreign affairs.

The institutional capacity to manage, coordinate, and execute national security includes much more than foreign policy and decisions about defense budgets. Force deployments, political and military commitments, intelligence, counterterrorism, public diplomacy, foreign broadcasting, trade policy, and economic sanctions are among the elements that require coordination and skilled implementation.[27] Recent experience provides cause for concern. The list includes shortcomings in intelligence coordination before and after 9/11, failure to plan effectively for the occupation of Iraq, inept public diplomacy, dysfunctional immigration policy, inadequate local, state, and national response to Hurricane Katrina, and haphazard federal government reaction to the BP-Deepwater Horizon oil spill in the Gulf of Mexico. These cases provide evidence that governmental capacity to manage large-scale challenges is sometimes badly flawed.

More broadly, this leads to the question of whether American institutions suffer from increasingly serious shortcomings in their ability to develop and implement effective policies at home and abroad. Bureaucracy, inefficiency, excessive regulation, political correctness, and the at times stupefying implementation of legal, environmental, liability,

---

[25] Christopher Gelpi, Peter Feaver, Jason Reifler, "Success Matters: Casualty Sensitivity and the War in Iraq," *International Security*, Vol. 30, No. 3 (Winter 2005/2006): 7–46, at 8.

[26] Aaron Friedberg, "The Long Haul: Fighting and Funding America's Next Wars," *Foreign Affairs*, Vol. 86, No. 4 (July/August 2007): 140–146.

[27] Dennis Ross makes this point in *Statecraft and How to Restore America's Standing in the World* (New York: Farrar, Straus and Giroux, 2007).

employment, and other rules can pose endless obstacles to even the most seemingly straightforward tasks. One author, Jonathan Rauch, has coined the term *demosclerosis* to describe these effects and the loss of public purpose that results. He points especially to the proliferation of interest groups, nongovernmental organizations, lobbies, and others who are attracted to the government's increasing role in taxing, regulating, subsidizing, and spending. The argument is compelling, though it is not new. Rauch's book was published in 1994, and it also draws on the earlier ideas of Mancur Olson, whose *Logic of Collective Action* dates from 1965.[28]

One can add to this catalog of governmental problems such matters as the proliferation in numbers of public employees and the expanding scope of regulation required in financial services and health care. For example, the financial reform law passed in 2010 runs to 2,319 pages and mandates numerous commissions and reporting requirements. In turn, the health care law passed by the same Congress is 2,409 pages long, and creates 183 new agencies, commissions, and panels.[29]

Examples such as these would seem to suggest impending paralysis in government, but it is here that another fundamental feature of American public life plays a countervailing role. At the national level, the core branches of government – the Congress, presidency, and judiciary – really do check and balance one another, a subject drilled into students even in elementary school. At least as important, if not more so, are the openness, flexibility, and adaptability of society and politics. These, combined with the structural features of federalism, so that fifty states and countless localities offer points of access for change, innovation, and political contestation, mean that the rules remain constantly in flux. The wave of deregulation that took place in the 1980s and 1990s provides such an illustration, as does the surge in popular reaction expressed in the Tea Party movement. These reactions can and do overshoot, but then themselves become objects of correction and redress. The broader and more important point is that the flexibility of society in itself provides an invaluable compensatory mechanism.

---

[28] Jonathan Rauch, *Demosclerosis: The Silent Killer of American Government* (New York: Crown, 1994). Also see Mancur Olson, *The Logic of Collective Action: Public Goods and the Theory of Groups* (Cambridge, MA: Harvard University Press, 1965).

[29] Based on an analysis by Robert E. Moffit of the Heritage Foundation, cited in David Brooks, "The Technocracy Boom," *The New York Times*, July 7, 2010.

It is also important to note that the American experience includes massive undertakings carried out with notable success. Among the most noteworthy cases is the extraordinary mobilization of manpower and industry at the outbreak of World War II. In just three and a half years after the December 1941 Japanese attack at Pearl Harbor, America successfully enlisted, trained, and armed huge forces, deployed its armies across vast oceans, fought and won a two-front war, and produced vast quantities of ships, tanks, and planes, arming not only itself, but its allies as well. By the end of the war, the U.S. army, navy, marines, and army air corps numbered twelve million men, the great majority of whom were then successfully demobilized and found education and productive jobs in the following years. An additional 350,000 women served in military non-combat roles in the Women's Army Auxiliary Corps (later, the WACs), Women Airforce Service Pilots (WASP), Women Accepted for Volunteer Military Services (WAVES), a branch of the Marines and Coast Guard (SPARS), and in the Army and Navy Nurse Corps.

Other examples of successful projects on a grand scale include the World War II Manhattan Project to develop the world's first atomic weapon; the Marshall Plan, which provided aid of monumental proportions to rebuild Europe and reinvigorate its economies in the early postwar period; the interstate highway program of the 1950s and 1960s; and the enormous expansion of higher education in the late 1950s and early 1960s. In response to the Soviet launching of Sputnik in 1957, there was President Kennedy's pledge to be the first country to send a man to the moon and to do so before the end of the 1960s. The Apollo project succeeded with this effort in 1969. A more recent example can be found in the initial post-9/11 action against the Taliban in Afghanistan. Within four weeks after the attack, U.S. Special Forces had begun military operations. By early December, utilizing cutting-edge military technology and air support, and in cooperation with the Afghan Northern Alliance, they had succeeded in defeating and ousting the regime that had provided shelter and backing for al-Qaeda. Precedents such as these provide impressive examples of how American governments have been able to develop the capability for effective response and at times have done so with extraordinary speed and efficiency.

The intangible, albeit indispensable, element of domestic capacity is public support and what the British author and historian Michael Howard has referred to as the social cohesion necessary for sustaining national power and strategy. As the Gelpi, Feaver, and Reifler's study discussed in this section suggests, the expectation of eventual success is critical. So too are political skills and leadership, as well as diplomatic adroitness in gaining support from other countries. Here, cooperation with allies becomes especially important in ways that go well beyond burden sharing because, in the eyes of American opinion leaders and the general public, it reinforces the legitimacy and acceptability of the action being taken.

There is one additional and often insufficiently appreciated element: the urgency of external threat. During the five decades from Pearl Harbor to the end of the Cold War, the United States faced profound challenges to its national security and vital interests, first from Nazi Germany and Imperial Japan and then, following a brief interlude, from the Soviet Union. The degree of domestic consensus about these threats, shared by the public, foreign policy elites, decision makers, political parties, and the media, provided the domestic foundation for a robust national security policy. This general consensus did not preclude domestic dissent and disagreement, let alone ensure unanimity of views, for example, in regard to the Vietnam War, but it did provide a basis for coherent and effective national action in mustering resources.

After World War II and the Cold War, the post–Cold War era (1991–2001) provided a marked contrast. In the absence of consensus about the existence of a profound overall threat, the salience of foreign policy dropped quite noticeably. Election exit polls during the 1990s found only single-digit percentages of voters identifying foreign or security policy as among the leading concerns shaping their votes. Television and newspaper treatment of foreign affairs plummeted, and attention to foreign policy issues during presidential and congressional election campaigns also declined. Together, these elements undermined the Clinton administration's ability to muster public and congressional support for its foreign policy initiatives.

The 9/11 attacks on New York and Washington brought a dramatically heightened sense of danger and a renewed urgency to world affairs. This attention nonetheless ebbed with the passage of time, increasing partisan acrimony, public disillusionment with the Iraq and Afghanistan wars, and the absence of another mass-casualty attack on American soil. That leaves a major uncertainty in any attempt to gauge the future domestic policy environment. In this instance, too, the reciprocal interrelationships and feedback loops between domestic and foreign policy come into play. Moreover, the possibility of a future mass-casualty attack within the United States continues, even though its probability is unknowable. Were such an attack to occur, it is certainly possible or even likely that there would be a resurgence of support for a very robust, even draconian, response and for paying whatever price was required to combat lethal adversaries.

Conversely, in the absence of another such attack and with widespread concern about the economy, domestic support for an interventionist or even actively engaged foreign policy is likely to lessen. Even so, voices calling for outright withdrawal or isolationism have remained limited. Illustratively, in the case of the 2008 presidential campaign, as in primaries during the previous several presidential election cycles, Republican and Democratic candidates arguing for a significantly curtailed global role were relegated to the political margins and did not become plausible contenders for their parties' presidential nominations. It is worth recalling that the 2008 major party nominees, John McCain and Barack Obama, both endorsed a leading world role for the United States, promising to carry out this task more successfully and with more support from international partners, while avoiding what they identified as mistakes of the Bush administration. At the time, the most commonly cited of these mistakes were said to be the terrorist detention facility at Guantanamo Bay, the treatment of detainees, and inadequate response to global climate change. Both candidates pledged to fight the war on terror more effectively, prevail against the Taliban and al-Qaeda in Afghanistan, oppose Iran's acquisition of nuclear weapons, support Israel, and work toward Middle East peace. They also favored increasing the size of the U.S. Army and Marine Corps, strengthening cooperation with Europe, supporting the admission of Georgia and Ukraine to NATO, and being prepared to intervene to combat genocide where possible.

In office, the Obama administration followed a mixed set of foreign policies. Its style and rhetoric conveyed an eagerness to negotiate and accommodate rather than confront. This was apparent in a determination to draw a line between itself and the Bush presidency, as evident, for example, in its initial reluctance to criticize China for predatory trade practices and manipulation of the exchange rate for the yuan. Not until its third year in office did the Obama administration become more assertive in its criticism of China's economic and foreign policy behavior. In this case, the Obama policy was constrained because of its dependence on China for the purchase of U.S. Treasury bills. The administration also made repeated and largely fruitless attempts to engage the Iranian regime in negotiations over its covert nuclear program, and it did not publicly confront Iran over its aid to insurgents in Iraq and Afghanistan, where Iranian Revolutionary Guard Corps (IRGC) training and weapons led to the deaths of American soldiers.

Challenges and Challengers

The domestic political foundations for the American era rest on attitudes, institutions, and policies. Public attitudes, although exuding pessimism over a sluggish economy, stubborn unemployment, and competition from China, nonetheless continue to reflect pride in America. This orientation also finds expression in a willingness to use force when vital national interests are at stake, a tolerance for military casualties, and a desire to retain American world leadership, though with an increased concern that power be used prudently. Neither elites nor the public want to see material resources, political influence, or human lives expended carelessly, let alone when other countries or institutions can and should take responsibility. Although public tolerance for frustrating and costly commitments in Iraq and Afghanistan has diminished, neither conflict ranked among the issues most important to voters at the time of the 2010 midterm elections. As noted in this chapter's section on public attitudes, only after nearly a decade of the Afghanistan conflict did a majority of Americans come to favor the withdrawal of troops as soon as possible.

Institutions bequeathed by the Founders display the strengths as well as the weaknesses long criticized by those who search for the underlying source of America's problems in its constitutional structure. These institutions themselves – though much discussed – do not differ markedly from what they were when the country's status as a superpower went largely unquestioned. The policy process is messy and at times chaotic and wasteful, and almost always open to pulling and hauling across region, interest, ideology, and party. But the frustrations and difficulties of leadership within the American system are nothing new – as Harry Truman observed six decades ago in regard to what would await the incoming President Eisenhower: "He'll sit here, and he'll say, 'Do this! Do that!' *And nothing will happen.* Poor Ike – it won't be a bit like the Army. He'll find it very frustrating."[30]

As the late Richard Neustadt noted in his classic work on the presidency, presidential power is the power to persuade.[31] Yet, despite the unwieldy nature of the political process, persuasion and leadership have been achievable for the implementation of major national policies as different as those of Presidents Woodrow Wilson, Franklin Roosevelt, Harry Truman, Lyndon Johnson, Ronald Reagan, Bill Clinton, and Barack Obama. These have occurred within the very same institutions that have served in good days and bad.

Ultimately, effective responses to the difficulties facing the United States depend on the beliefs, strategies, and policies of political elites and the attitudes and reactions of the public. This may seem to downplay the difficulty of contemporary domestic issues, especially economic and structural challenges, but America's underlying advantages remain impressive. Here, the words of a dispassionate and clear-eyed foreign observer, *The Economist* newspaper of London, provide a striking contrast to widespread but facile pessimism:

Despite its problems, America has far more going for it than its current mood suggests. It is still the most innovative economy on earth, the place where the world's greatest universities meet the world's deepest pockets. Its demography is favourable, with a high birth rate and limitless space into which to expand. It has a flexible and hard-working labour force. Its ultra-low bond yields are a sign that the world's investors still think it a good long-term bet. The most enterprising individuals on earth still clamour to come to America.[32]

The list of strengths can readily be expanded. For example, with reference to immigration, successive waves of newcomers have enriched

---

[30] Richard E. Neustadt, *Presidential Power, the Politics of Leadership* (New York: John Wiley & Sons, 1960), p. 9.
[31] Ibid.
[32] *The Economist*, October 28, 2010.

the country, stimulated its growth, and provided a source of innovation and dynamism. This absorptive capacity has been an exceptional feature of the United States and even now sets it apart from virtually every major country in the world.

Moreover, American English has become the international lingua franca. It is characteristically the means by which international business is conducted, by which science, the Internet, and international aviation take place, and the second language through which those in different foreign lands communicate. Its ubiquity provides subtle but real advantages to the United States.

The foremost challenge to be tackled remains the combined burden of the national debt, annual deficits, and the rising tide of entitlement costs as the Baby Boomer generation begins to retire. To cope with these financial problems is necessary and difficult, but it is not an insurmountable task. As Tocqueville reminds us, the United States has repeatedly demonstrated the ability to "repair" its "faults." Of course, past accomplishments provide no guarantee about the future, and an effective response demands wise policies, skillful leadership, and a sufficient political consensus to achieve needed outcomes. A major element in any calculation concerns the scale of available resources. Some of the most threatening scenarios imply that negative results are already locked in. However, projections in estimates for U.S. GDP by the year 2020 vary by as much as $3 *trillion*, depending on whether during the intervening years the economy matches high or low growth scenarios. Different outcomes will have an enormous effect on federal revenues, since tax receipts are closely related to national income, and stronger economic growth would make an enormous difference in the financial "repair" tasks facing the country. These differences, along with the long list of things America has "going for it" and the country's historical resilience, provide a reminder as to why we should be skeptical about pessimistic predictions concerning the American future and any notion that decline is already "baked into the cake."

4

Threats to Persistent Primacy and the Rise of Others

"A world without U.S. primacy will be a world with more violence and disorder and less democracy and economic growth than a world where the United States continues to have more influence than any other country in shaping global affairs. The sustained international primacy of the U.S. is central to the welfare and security of Americans and to the future of freedom, democracy, open economies, and international order in the world."

– Samuel H. Huntington[1]

Arguments about the American era at home and abroad involve two propositions. Those who make the case for American decline assert, first, that the United States itself as a society, an economy, and a political power is weakening or has even become enfeebled; and second, that its international primacy is ebbing because of the rise of other powers. Previous chapters have focused on the domestic basis for American power and influence. This chapter now turns to the international dimension. In doing so, it is essential to think broadly, rigorously, and long-term, yet it is sobering to consider how varied and volatile previous and even recent assessments have been. Observers at home and abroad have periodically offered pessimistic and even dire assertions about America. In hindsight, after many years or often after even a very brief interval, these predictions have proved to be far too

[1] "Why International Primacy Matters," *International Security*, Vol. 17, No. 4 (Spring 1993): 68–93, at 83.

pessimistic, even embarrassingly so. In seeking to make sense of threats to American primacy, whether in terms of the diffusion of power or the more direct types of external dangers or internal weaknesses, many in the political world, the academy, and the media have fallen prey to the declinist temptation.

Elusive Dangers: Volatility in Threat Assessment

Long-term predictions are notoriously hard to get right. Samuel Huntington famously identified no fewer than five waves of declinism in a period of little more than two decades: in 1957–1958, after the Soviet launch of Sputnik, the world's first space satellite; at the end of the 1960s, when President Nixon proclaimed the end of the bipolar world; in 1973–1974, as a result of the Arab oil embargo and the staggering increase in world oil prices; in the late 1970s, after Vietnam, Watergate, and Soviet inroads in the developing world as well as expansion of their nuclear forces; and in 1987, with budget and trade deficits, the financial threat from Japan, and an October 1987 stock market crash.[2]

Consider, however, just the three most recent decades: the last ten years of the Cold War, the post–Cold War decade, and the post-9/11 decade. Within each of these periods, assessments of the United States have varied sharply, whether expressed in terms of America's extraordinary power and influence or, conversely, in regard to its vulnerability and potential weakness.

The 1980s began with widespread pessimism in the face of economic and geopolitical rivalry abroad. Japan had mounted an enormous challenge in its export-led growth and industrial competitiveness, while the United States struggled with its worst economic crisis since the 1930s, combining a severe recession, record postwar unemployment, serious inflation, and interest rates as high as 18 percent. The effects of America's 1975 withdrawal from Indochina and the fall of Vietnam, Laos, and Cambodia to communist forces were still widely felt. Soviet-supported movements had made major inroads in Angola, Ethiopia, Mozambique, Nicaragua, and Yemen, and Soviet troops occupied

---

[2] Samuel P. Huntington, "The U.S. – Decline or Renewal?" *Foreign Affairs*, Vol. 67, No. 2 (Winter 1988/1989): 76 and 94–95.

Afghanistan. The Shah of Iran had been overthrown and replaced by an anti-American Islamist regime. The U.S. embassy in Teheran had been seized by student radicals who, with the backing of the mullahs, held fifty-five embassy personnel hostage for 444 days. The United States had lost its nuclear superiority vis-à-vis the Soviets, and Marxist-Leninist ideologues had begun to speak of a shift in the "correlation of forces," that is, a fundamental transformation in the world balance of geopolitical power. In this environment, no less a figure than George Kennan, the father of the containment doctrine (even though for much of the postwar era, a disgruntled critic of American policy at home and abroad), could write in 1984 that the United States was "a politically unsuccessful and tragic country... always vulnerable to abuse and harassment at the hands of the dominant forces of the moment."[3]

Economic turmoil, reaction to reversals abroad, and loss of confidence in the Carter presidency led to the election of Ronald Reagan in 1980. With economic recovery, an upbeat theme ("It's morning in America again"), and a weak Democratic opponent, Reagan swept to reelection in 1984, winning forty-nine states. While the second Reagan term saw a major easing of the Cold War, by 1987 the foreign economic competition (noted earlier in this section) gave rise to a renewed burst of declinism. Among others, Paul Kennedy's 1987 book, *The Rise and Fall of the Great Powers*, emerged at just the right time to ride this latest wave of pessimism. Kennedy's argument suggested that, as in the case of great powers of the past, most recently Great Britain, the United States was about to experience the effects of imperial overstretch, in which foreign and military commitments exceeded the country's capacity.[4] Despite the dire forecast, the decade ended not with America's demise, but with the opening of the Berlin Wall and end of the Cold War.

The start of the 1990s brought the dissolution of the Soviet bloc, the collapse of communism, and the breakup of the Soviet Union. In

---

[3] Quoted in Mark Atwood Lawrence, "The Heart of a Realist," *The New York Times Book Review*, July 25, 2010.

[4] Paul Kennedy, *The Rise and Fall of the Great Powers: Economic Change and Military Conflict from 1500 to 2000* (New York: Random, 1987). Also David P. Calleo, *Beyond American Hegemony* (New York: Basic Books, 1987). For a counterpoint published three years later, which was much less pessimistic, see Joseph S. Nye, *Bound to Lead: The Changing Nature of American Power* (New York: Basic Books, 1990).

1991, backed by an unprecedented UN Security Council resolution, the United States successfully led an impressive international coalition in the defeat of Iraqi president Saddam Hussein's forces and their ouster from Kuwait – all with "miraculously light" American casualties. In the wake of these events, treatments of America's world role, which only a few years earlier had forecast gloom, shifted to descriptions of the United States as the lone superpower, not just in military and geopolitical terms, but also with respect to the triumph of the American model of market capitalism and liberal democracy.[5] As the decade wore on, the "Washington consensus" was trumpeted as both the model and the only viable course for countries wishing to meet the needs of their people for economic and social development and prosperity.[6] By the middle of the decade, the overwhelming character of American primacy across the multiple dimensions by which world power is measured had become a given – not only on the part of those who embraced it, but also by critics who pointed with alarm at this predominance and its implications.

Especially in the academic world – but not only there – the end of the Cold War and the appearance of a seemingly unipolar era gave rise to proclamations of a "new world order," in which traditional security concerns were increasingly outmoded. The phrase was most notably used by President George H. W. Bush, in a March 1991 speech following the success of Operation Desert Storm. But the idea was amplified in post–Cold War discourse among academics, public intellectuals, and foreign observers, who emphasized the "new" security issues such as civilian power, development, globalization, disease, the environment, and national and cultural identity as the predominant concerns in world affairs. International institutions and global governance became the framework for this discourse. In the meantime, traditional security concerns were increasingly labeled as "old thinking."

The sobering reality of the 1990s, however, was that power remained very much a matter of life and death. The ability of the UN Security Council to arrive at a common position on the use of force to remove Saddam Hussein from Kuwait provided not the harbinger of a

---

[5] Francis Fukuyama, "The End of History," *The National Interest*, Vol. 16 (Summer 1989): 3–18.

[6] For example, Thomas Friedman's reference to the "golden straitjacket," in his best seller, *The Lexus and the Olive Tree* (New York: Farrar, Straus and Giroux, 1999).

new global order but a rare exception. Instead, ethnic cleansing, civil wars, and the consequences of state failure became brutally apparent in places such as Somalia, Bosnia, Rwanda, the Congo, and Kosovo. A graphic illustration of this took place in the Bosnian Muslim community of Srebrenica in July 1995. There, in what the Security Council had declared a "safe area," presided over by a battalion of Dutch troops wearing blue helmets, driving white-painted vehicles, and under a UN flag, the flawed assumptions about global governance were lethally exposed. While the Dutch stood by, Serb militias overran the town and in the course of several days rounded up and deliberately executed at least 7,000 Bosnian Muslim men and boys. The lesson here and often elsewhere was that the alternative to serious leadership or involvement by the United States in urgent and deadly crises was not that the UN, some other multilateral institution, or another powerful state would take the lead in maintaining order, but that the alternative was more likely to be inaction and often tragedy.

At the same time, insufficient attention was paid to a different kind of gathering threat. In this case, indications of radical jihadist terrorism were increasingly apparent but were not accorded the priority they deserved. Ominous signs were there: in the 1993 truck bombing at the World Trade Center, the 1996 suicide truck bombings of the U.S. embassies in Kenya and Tanzania, the October 2000 attack on the USS Cole in Yemen, and in Osama bin Laden's 1996 declaration of jihad against Americans, Israelis, and what he labeled the "Judeo-Crusader alliance."[7] The terrorist attacks were by no means ignored, but they did not become an overriding national security priority. Much more common as an expression of the decade's optimism about globalization was the sentiment voiced by President Bill Clinton: "In the new century, liberty will be spread by cell phone and cable modem."[8]

The shock of the September 11, 2001 attacks against the World Trade Center and the Pentagon defined much of the following decade for the United States, but – yet again – in successively contradictory terms. The ouster of the Taliban regime within months of the attack,

---

[7] Declaration of Jihad, August 23, 1996, in Bruce Lawrence (ed.), *Messages to the World: The Statements of Osama bin Laden* (New York: Verso, 2005), pp. 23–30.

[8] Quoted by Fouad Ajami, "The New Faith," *Saisphere*, alumni magazine of the Johns Hopkins University School of Advanced International Studies (Washington, DC: 2000), p. 13.

followed less than eighteen months later by the invasion of Iraq and the quick defeat and demise of Saddam Hussein, gave rise to awed statements about America's unparalleled power. The widely quoted words of Paul Kennedy – "Nothing has ever existed like this disparity of power; nothing" – typified these sentiments.[9]

Not everyone shared Kennedy's (then) adulation, and the Bush administration itself became a lightning rod for criticism, even before the March 2003 invasion of Iraq. For example, as early as July 2001, a prominent British journalist, Polly Toynbee, could write that Europe was "now faced with a reckless brigand in command of the only superpower."[10] The remark – expressed not only prior to Iraq, but even before Afghanistan – reflected not so much a reasoned debate about American power, but a visceral reaction against the seemingly overwhelming predominance of the United States as well as toward the Bush presidency and persona.

Admiring – or disparaging – depictions of the United States at the pinnacle of world power did not outlast the decade. Growing insurgencies in Iraq and Afghanistan, rising American and allied casualties, and the failure to cope effectively with Hurricane Katrina, which devastated New Orleans in August 2005, stimulated a shift in perceptions. The United States no longer seemed omnipotent. In turn, 2007 saw the bursting of the real estate bubble and then September 2008, the collapse of Lehman Brothers and the eruption of a full-blown financial crisis. Instead of being seen as the "hyperpower," America was increasingly portrayed in almost dire terms. Commentators and pundits shifted rapidly, no longer describing America as uniquely dominant and powerful but instead vulnerable and imperiled. As an example of this volatility, Eric Edelman has pointed to the sharp contrast between the 2004 report of the National Intelligence Council, *Mapping the Global Future 2020*, which saw unipolarity as likely to remain a persistent feature in world affairs, and the 2008 publication, *Global Trends 2025*, which forecast a quite different global multipolar system.[11]

---

[9] "The Eagle Has Landed," *Financial Times*, February 1, 2002.
[10] *The Guardian*, July 18, 2001.
[11] See Eric S. Edelman, *Understanding America's Contested Primacy* (Washington, DC: Center for Strategic and Budgetary Assessments, 2010), pp. 2–3.

Even the 2008 Obama election victory, which was widely embraced abroad, did not stem the flood of pessimistic assessments. These intensified after huge Democratic losses in the 2010 midterm election, the worst since 1938. A leading political journalist declared that "in this election you can glimpse the brutish future of American politics,"[12] while a domestic critic, John Judis, expressed the mood on the left by proclaiming, "What this election suggests to me is that the United States may have finally lost its ability to adapt politically to the systemic crises that it has periodically faced."[13] On the day after the election, a British political scientist wrote the *Financial Times* to cite America's "inevitable relative decline" and to warn against the danger of the United States becoming "more and more divided and unstable."[14]

As noted in Chapter 1, these expressions of extraordinary primacy and then of radical decline juxtapose two forms of hyperbole. The abrupt shift in views reflects enormous overstatement – in awe during the earlier part of the decade and in exaggerated depictions of weakness and incapacity in the latter part. Neither view was sufficiently nuanced or reflective, let alone an adequate basis for appreciating the character of American power, and both embodied the pervasive tendency toward overstated reactions to immediate events.

Thinking about Threats

What can we say about the future of the American era at home and abroad that has any hope of being more durable than so many of the short-lived predictions and assessments of recent decades? A requirement here is to differentiate between two broadly different types of foreign threat. The first of these concerns the rise of others and the resultant diffusion of American power in a world where more and more states matter. A second type of challenge is more direct. It

---

[12] Thomas B. Edsall, "Limited War: How the Age of Austerity Will Remake American Politics," *The New Republic*, October 20, 2010.

[13] John B. Judis, "Here Comes Our Lost Generation: The Consequences of a Richly Deserved Defeat," *The New Republic Daily*, November 3, 2010, http://www.tnr.com/article/politics/78890/a-lost generation, accessed November 6, 2010.

[14] Prof. Philip G. Cerny, "Decline has fuelled paranoia and the Tea Party," letter to the *Financial Times*, November 3, 2010.

concerns threats either from hostile states or from non-state actors such as al-Qaeda.

In terms of the first of these challenges, there have been subtle and not-so-subtle shifts in the international distribution of power. One of these changes is the erosion in the standing of America's principal allies among the market democracies, as Europe and Japan have weakened in their economic performance, their share of world output, and their military capabilities. Meanwhile, other regional states have acquired increased power and prominence, as measured by their growing economic weight and geopolitical presence, and are less inclined to follow America's lead. The rise of China is prominently cited, but other developing countries are also increasing in importance. For example, the contrary stance taken by Brazil and Turkey on the Iranian nuclear issue, not just in opposition to the American-led call for sanctions, but to the position of all five permanent members of the UN Security Council, suggests the unwieldy and disparate character of twenty-first-century international politics. The implication for the United States is that compared to the unipolar status it possessed in the years after the end of the Cold War, it now faces a more diverse and difficult international environment.

As for more direct threats, terrorism, cyber attacks, and the proliferation of nuclear weapons, as well as other weapons of mass destruction (chemical, biological, and radiological), pose physical dangers. Mass-casualty terrorism, as was dramatically evident on 9/11, is an obvious illustration of this kind of peril, but in the coming years, missiles and weapons of mass destruction are likely to pose a growing danger to America's interests and allies abroad as well as within the United States itself. Since the end of the Cold War, the importance of strategic nuclear weapons has widely been discounted or even treated as a relic of an earlier era. Yet depictions of "nuclear zero" as an ultimate and even achievable goal are manifestly unrealistic. This is not only a matter of Russia's evolving modernization of its seriously diminished arsenal, but of China, North Korea, Iran, and possibly others, with their own active nuclear programs.

In assessing foreign threats, the nature of American power needs to be taken into account, especially in order to avoid measuring current strength against an imaginary yardstick of past dominance. It is tempting to point to any number of areas (trade, economic policy, sanctions, and the environment) in order to argue that failure to prevail provides proof of decline. While its superpower status and even primacy during the past seven decades gave the United States unusual influence and made it more likely that other states would be receptive to American policies and preferences, there was never anything inevitable about the ability to determine outcomes. Power is not identical with influence, and even at the very height of its power, America's ability to achieve desired results was never a foregone conclusion. This was not only true in dealing with hostile powers, but even in relation to allies such as France.

Consider a number of the more serious reversals experienced by the United States since the end of World War II. These included the Chinese Communist victory over the American-backed Nationalists in 1949; the Korean War (1950–1953) ending in a stalemate, with 37,000 American dead; the Cuban Revolution in 1959 and the failure of the CIA-organized Bay of Pigs operation in 1961. The years that followed witnessed numerous strains among allies over economic, trade, and military matters, including French president Charles de Gaulle's veto of Britain's Common Market application and his withdrawal of France from the NATO integrated military command; the October 1973 Arab oil embargo; the Vietnam War, with 58,000 Americans killed and the Communist North Vietnamese defeat of the South Vietnamese government in 1975; and the Iranian revolution in 1979, with the overthrow of the Shah and the subsequent U.S. embassy hostage crisis. October 1993 saw the "Blackhawk Down" incident in Somalia, leaving eighteen Army Rangers and Delta Force soldiers dead and leading to American withdrawal six months later. In turn, the 21st Century brought the 9/11 attack on New York and Washington. Each of these reversals or even outright defeats occurred during the years in which American power was supposedly at its zenith. Keeping these experiences in mind can be useful in order to avoid unrealistic expectations about what international primacy entails, as well as to avoid exaggerated pessimism in reaction to contemporary problems.

We should also be wary of condescending attitudes about the United States itself, its political system, its politics, and its people. As noted in the previous chapter, the cut and thrust of partisan debate is nothing new and can be seen even in bitter arguments among the Founders. While serious errors of policy and delays in coming to grips with domestic and foreign crises are nothing new, the long-term record of the United States is one of remarkable resilience, adaptation, and crisis response. Hence the sweeping diatribes delivered periodically by critics should be met with considerable skepticism. George Kennan's "unsuccessful and tragic country" is but one example. Much more recent illustrations can be found in the condescending comment by Stephen Walt of Harvard that "We are a nation of swaggering sheep,"[15] and in the sweeping assertion by Zbigniew Brezinski that "most Americans are close to total ignorance about the world. They are ignorant."[16]

The Rise of Others

Descriptions of the world as becoming multipolar are by no means new. President Richard Nixon in his *TIME* magazine "Man of the Year" interview of January 1972 described what he saw as the emergence of a balance among five principal centers of power: the United States, the Soviet Union, China, Western Europe, and Japan.[17] This conception, widely cited at the time, proved to be premature. Only the United States and the USSR were military superpowers, and among the five power centers cited, only the United States was both a military and an economic superpower. Moreover, despite an emerging détente between Washington and Moscow, the Cold War was not over and would continue and at times even intensify until the end of the following decade. Even so, the array of actors and agendas had already greatly expanded from what it had been at the close of World War II and in the 1950s.

With the end of the Cold War, many authors and pundits, especially academic and political realists, predicted that the collapse of the Soviet Union and a period of unipolarity, with the United States as the sole superpower, would trigger balancing behavior. Yet despite these expectations, real balancing did not take place. There was no

---

[15] Stephen M. Walt, "A Nation of Swaggering Sheep," *Foreignpolicy.com*, January 4, 2010.

[16] "Ex-National Security Advisor Zbigniew Brzezinski: Spokespersons of US Right 'In Most Cases Stunningly Ignorant'," *Spiegel Online*, December 6, 2010, http://www.spiegel.de/international/world/0,1518,733079,00.html, accessed December 7, 2010.

[17] *TIME*, January 3, 1972.

true coalition formation undertaken by other powers aimed at countering the power of the United States or arming themselves in pursuit of balance, let alone deliberately preparing for the possibility of war. And even a decade later, the bitter reaction to the American-led intervention in Iraq and the intense diplomatic opposition of France, Germany, and Russia did not stimulate the creation of such a coalition, despite repeated predictions that the time for real counterbalancing had at last arrived.

In the case of the Europeans, French president Jacques Chirac and German chancellor Gerhard Schroeder could not speak for the majority of their EU partners, and in the early months of 2003, on the eve of the American-led intervention against Saddam Hussein, some two-thirds of the member governments of both the EU and NATO supported the Bush administration's fateful decision.[18] Despite arguments about "soft-balancing,"[19] not only did balancing not occur, but principal European leaders either maintained (as in the case of Britain) or reasserted (in the case of Germany and France) pragmatic Atlanticist policies, while the largest EU member states mostly continued to be governed by avowedly Atlanticist presidents or prime ministers. For its part, the EU did not distance itself from the United States, let

---

[18] Leaders of the Czech Republic, Denmark, Hungary, Italy, Poland, and Portugal signed a letter by Prime Ministers Blair of Britain and Aznar of Spain. A similar letter was signed by ten members of the Vilnius group: Albania, Bulgaria, Croatia, Estonia, Latvia, Lithuania, Macedonia, Romania, Slovakia, and Slovenia. The Netherlands, Iceland, and Turkey also contributed to the Iraq war coalition. For an official list of the forty-seven countries supporting the Operation Iraqi Freedom coalition as of March 27, 2003, see: http://www.whitehouse.gov/news/releases/2003/03/print/20030327-10.html

[19] For example, Kenneth Waltz had argued that friends as well as foes would seek to balance against the international predominance of the United States, in "The Emerging Structure of International Politics," *International Security*, Vol. 17, No. 4 (Spring 1993): 5–51. Also Waltz, "Globalization and Governance," *PS: Political Science and Politics*, Vol. 32, No. 4 (December 1999): 693-700; Christopher Layne, "The Unipolar Illusion Revisited: The Coming End of the United States' Unipolar Moment," *International Security*, Vol. 31, No. 2 (Fall 2006): 7–41; and Robert A. Pape, "Soft Balancing against the United States," *International Security*, Vol. 30, No. 1 (Summer 2005): 7–45. Others effectively rebutted the argument. See Keir A. Lieber and Gerard Alexander, "Waiting For Balancing: Why the World Is Not Pushing Back," *International Security*, Vol. 30, No. 1 (Summer 2003): 109–139; and Stephen G. Brooks and William C. Wohlforth, "Hard Times for Soft Balancing," *International Security*, Vol. 30, No. 1 (Summer 2003): 72–108.

alone emerge as a strategic competitor.[20] There were and remain good reasons for this long-term continuity. These include not only shared interests and values, but also the inability of EU member countries to create genuine political unity and a military force with sufficient funding, advanced technology, power projection, and unity of command that would enable it to play a role in the security realm that Europe's size, population, and wealth would otherwise dictate.

While true power balancing did not take place, there is no doubt that some four decades after Nixon's pronouncement about multipolarity, and more than two decades after the end of the Cold War, the cast of relevant regional and world powers has greatly expanded. This can be seen not only in data about trade and economic growth, but explicitly in the enlargement of the G-7 group of advanced economies to become the G-20. The original group began in 1975 with summit meetings among the leading industrial countries and was then formalized as an organization in 1985. At the time it included only Britain, Canada, France, Germany, Italy, Japan, and the United States. Its members gathered annually to address shared economic and sometimes political concerns. They began to invite Russia to a number of their meetings in the 1990s, and in 1998 established the G-8 as a means of formally including Russia, even though on some subjects they continued to limit their meetings to the original G-7 countries. In 1999, in response to the intensified pace of globalization, the burgeoning of world trade and finance, and the growing importance of developing countries, they expanded to become the G-20, adding to their membership Argentina, Australia, Brazil, China, the EU, India, Indonesia, Mexico, Saudi Arabia, South Africa, South Korea, and Turkey.

The rise of these and other countries, especially in Asia, the Middle East, and Latin America, certainly represents a further diffusion of power. In particular, the BRICS (Brazil, Russia, India, China, and South Africa) are pointed to as embodying the emergence of major regional powers as important international actors. Among the BRICS,

---

[20] For example, Charles Kupchan had proclaimed that NATO "is soon to be defunct." See "The Waning Days of the Atlantic Alliance," in Bertel Heurlin and Mikkel Vedby Rasmussen (eds.), *Challenges and Capabilities: NATO in the 21st Century* (Copenhagen: Danish Institute for International Studies, 2003), p. 25.

Russia is mainly relevant to its immediate neighbors, over whom it seeks to regain influence and even domination, and as an energy and arms exporter, but it is by no means a vibrant economic and political actor. Brazil, India, China, and the others making up the G-20 are more noteworthy, and the symbolism of the BRICS label mainly pertains to them.

There is, however, a certain mystique about these states and the expanding role they play in world affairs. Some liberal international-ist and globalist thinkers claim that this heralds not only a profound diffusion of power, but a global transition in which the U.S. role will be much diminished, to be replaced by a multiplicity of actors, most prominently China, operating through transformed international insti-tutions reshaped to give them much more influence and the institutions themselves much greater authority in a globalized world. For example, the Princeton political scientist John Ikenberry, who had previously written that "the most powerful and rich countries in the world are now all democracies" (somehow managing to overlook the reality of authoritarianism in China and Russia),[21] now sees the BRICS working with the United States and Europe to revise, adapt, and strengthen the institutions of global governance. This is said to be happening because these countries have benefitted so much from the global order created by the United States after World War II, including the UN, the World Bank, the International Monetary Fund, the General Agreement on Tariffs and Trade, and the American-led alliance structure, but which is now in serious need of updating and revision.

Notwithstanding the belief that "the continuing rise of economic and security interdependence is creating new incentives for the expan-sion of institutionalized cooperation,"[22] the actual performance of the BRICS suggests not a benign, cooperative orientation toward strengthening global governance, but a far more self-interested and less

---

[21] G. John Ikenberry, "Liberal International Theory in the Wake of 911 and American Unipolarity," paper prepared for seminar on "IR Theory, Unipolarity and September 11th – Five Years On," NUPI, Oslo, Norway, February 3–4, 2006, http://www.princeton.edu/~gji3/Microsoft_Word_-_Ikenberry-Liberal-International-Theory-in-the-Wake-of-911-and-American-unipoliarity-Oslo-word%20doc.pdf, accessed November 25, 2010.

[22] G. John Ikenberry, "A Crisis of Global Governance?" *Current History* (November 2010): 315–321, at 321. Also see Ikenberry, "The Future of the Liberal World Order: Internationalism after America," *Foreign Affairs* (May/June 2011): 56–68.

collaborative set of attitudes and policies across a wide range of economic, political, and security issues. For example, India was a key obstacle to successful completion of the Doha round of world trade liberalization, which failed to secure a new major international agreement to lower trade barriers.

In environmental policy, an especially vital concern for those focused on global governance, the experience of the November 2009 Copenhagen conference was shocking. A meeting meant to move the world beyond the Kyoto agreement toward a new binding accord on global climate change was instead marked by disarray. Key BRICS countries, especially China and India, rejected potential limits on their carbon emissions as harmful to their own economic development. Excluding the EU countries, which had been the principal backers of a new agreement, they met in a closed session, to which the United States belatedly gained admission, and agreed only on a loose statement of purpose.

Human rights mark another area in which the BRICS and other emerging regional powers have not only refused to cooperate but often have provided support to notorious violators. Invoking anti-colonialist loyalties, South Africa dragged its feet on sanctioning the brutal regime of President Robert Mugabe, which has reduced Zimbabwe to ruin, even while other African states pressed for action. India has collaborated with the corrupt and dictatorial rulers of neighboring energy- and timber-producing Myanmar (Burma). Turkey and Brazil opposed sanctions on Iran for its illegal and covert nuclear program, despite condemnation by the UN Security Council and the International Atomic Energy Agency (IAEA). Russia has repeatedly applied pressure on its neighbors, especially the former republics of the Soviet Union, using energy leverage, including interruptions of natural gas delivery during winter, as well as covert means through its foreign intelligence service, the FSB (successor to the notorious KGB).

Most notably of all, China has had a deplorable record on global governance issues. It supported the brutal regime of President al-Bashir in the Sudan, where it has key energy contracts, and has either obstructed or minimized international efforts to address proliferation and human rights issues in North Korea, Zimbabwe, Burma, Iran, and elsewhere. Together with Russia it vetoed UN Security Council condemnation of Syria for its murderous brutality against anti-government protestors. Citing its opposition to anything intruding on national sovereignty, China has had no qualms about reaching energy and trade deals with notorious regimes, even when these were the target of agreed on international sanctions. Moreover, China has pursued blatant mercantilist policies in trade and investment, manipulating the value of its currency by holding the yuan at artificially low levels in order to promote exports. It has proved predatory in its pursuit of energy and raw materials, failed to enforce intellectual property agreements, withheld key raw material exports as a political weapon (rare earths for Japan, needed for advanced electronics), and broken the rules of the World Trade Organization whenever it saw its own interests at stake.

The implications of these and other comparable cases are quite striking. On the environment, human rights, proliferation, and a variety of trade and investment issues, the BRICS for the most part are not embracing cooperative behavior or showing a willingness to contribute toward global order unless their own immediate self-interest makes this beneficial. As Walter Russell Mead has argued, the BRICS are unlikely to be accommodating toward liberal internationalism:

[T]he decline of two of the three Trilateral powers (Europe and Japan; the United States is in a different category) means that we increasingly live in a post-Trilateral world, and that world is much less hospitable to institutions and ideas that are rooted in the Kantian visions that have been so influential in European and American history.... Both because Europeans (and whites generally) are over-represented in the existing global institutions and because the institutions themselves evolved out of the era of western colonial dominance along western ideological and cultural patterns, the liberal internationalist vision has a limited appeal in countries like India and China."[23]

Thus as the relative weight of Europe and Japan has ebbed, the international economy is becoming less rather than more manageable. At the same time, the BRICS and others are making international institutions more unwieldy. Moreover, as Daniel Drezner observes,

[23] Walter Russell Mead, "Liberal Internationalism: The Twilight of a Dream," *The American Interest Online*, April 1, 2010.

the multiplicity of international organizations and regimes of all kinds is actually leading toward fewer binding rules in the global arena.[24]

The U.S. position thus remains unique. It has been the world's principal supporter of global governance through its leadership in the international economy, in promoting a liberal trading and monetary order, in security, in sustaining freedom of the seas and the global commons, and in creating and maintaining institutions. No country or institution is emerging to play the kind of role the United States has played in creating and sustaining key international institutions, and none is likely to do so in the foreseeable future. Hence the consequences of a lesser American role or even outright disengagement would mean not that other countries would become more engaged and supportive, but that these bodies and the shared forms of global order would be more likely to erode.

The Rise of China

Arguments about American decline inevitably rest in large part on assumptions about the rise of China. Observers marvel at its extraordinary economic dynamism, formidable export-led growth, and massive modernization and development projects. They are awed with China's sheer size, appetite for resources, ruthless competitive behavior, growing geopolitical influence, and potential to surpass the United States as the world's leading power. Examples of these reactions abound among foreign and domestic political leaders, strategists, commentators, and the wider public, as well as in books, magazines, newspapers, the Internet, and the broadcast media. As but one among countless examples, *The Wall Street Journal* devoted the entire front page of one of its Weekend sections to a depiction by Harvard historian Niall Ferguson of the PRC's momentum, the trajectory for its implicitly inevitable rise, and the "end of 500 years of Western predominance."[25]

---

[24] Daniel W. Drezner, "The Tragedy of the Global Institutional Commons," The Fletcher School, Tufts University, January 2009, http://graduateinstitute.ch/webdav/ site/ctei/shared/CTEI/3413/Fuzzy-Borders-Drezner.pdf, accessed December 8, 2010.
[25] Niall Ferguson, "In China's Orbit," *The Wall Street Journal*, November 20–21, 2010.

For some commentators, the blend of admiration and trepidation is mixed with concern about China's assertive mercantilism, its currency manipulation, its systematic intellectual piracy of advanced Western technology, its human rights abuses, and its increasingly predatory behavior. China scholar Edward Friedman of the University of Wisconsin finds that China's ruling groups first and foremost see the United States as an adversary.[26] This view leads to the broader question of whether a rising and increasingly powerful China will be content to take its place as a leading actor within the rules and institutions of a global order from which it has benefitted and that has made its own rise possible. Or, alternatively, will China instead prove as disruptive as a rising Imperial Germany was a century ago, aggressively asserting itself in ways that overturn the established order and spark conflict and even war?

On this point, Aaron Friedberg cites the past history of rising powers and their relations with existing dominant ones. Other than the case of the United States and Britain at the start of the twentieth century, the record is one of conflict. He cites Germany and Britain prior to World War I, Japan and the United States prior to World War II, and the United States and the USSR after 1945. Each of these cases led to arms races and hot or cold wars. Friedberg's sobering conclusion is that, "unless China undergoes a fundamental transformation in the character of its regime, there is good reason to worry about where its rivalry with the United States will lead."[27]

Some argue that China's self-interest in economic growth and in meeting the development needs of its own vast population will lead it to emphasize an orderly and non-disruptive path. Others point to the need for the ruling Communist Party to justify its continued autocratic rule by playing to nationalist and xenophobic sentiments among an otherwise more educated and aware population. The role of a rapidly modernizing and well-armed Peoples' Liberation Army may also intensify

---

[26] Edward Friedman, "Power Transition Theory: A Challenge to the Peaceful Rise of World Power China," in Herbert Yee (ed.), *China's Rise: Threat or Opportunity* (London: Routledge, 2011), pp. 11–32.

[27] Aaron L. Friedberg, "Future Course: Are the United States and China on a Collision Course?" *The New Republic*, May 26, 2011. Also see Friedberg, *A Contest for Supremacy: China, America, and the Struggle for Mastery in Asia* (New York: Norton, 2011).

this dynamic, as the PRC has been increasing its defense budget at the rate of 10 percent or more per year for the past two decades.

Yet any assessment of China needs to be made with some care. For one thing, as noted in Chapter 2, some of the foreboding bears an uncanny resemblance to worries about Japan a mere two decades ago. From today's vantage point, with Japan mired in economic stagnation and debt since the early 1990s, those earlier warnings have proved to be unduly alarmist. At the time, however, trade and economic data as well as inflammatory statements by prominent Japanese seemed to provide good reason for anxiety. For example, at the end of the 1980s, Akio Morita, a co-founder and then head of Sony, and Shintaro Ishihara, a leading politician and former Japanese cabinet minister, authored a controversial and widely circulated book entitled *The Japan That Can Say No.* In it, Morita proclaimed, "We are going to have a totally new configuration in the balance of power in the world," and Ishihara observed, "There is no hope for the U.S." He also proclaimed "the end of the modern era as developed by white Westerners."[28]

Indeed, as recently as 1993, the late Samuel Huntington, one of America's most original and highly regarded strategic thinkers, wrote that "Japanese strategy is a strategy of economic warfare," and he listed the reasons for his concern.[29] These included dangers to U.S. national security as Japan expanded its lead in key military technologies, rising Japanese economic power as a threat to the well-being of Americans, a resultant decline of U.S. influence in other countries, dangerous dependence on imports and funding from Japan, and Tokyo's attempts to influence policy in Washington, along with its measures to "cultivate" intellectuals and scholars at leading universities.

Granted, China today is more formidable than was Japan, but it remains essential to assess China's vulnerabilities as well as its impressive strengths. These vulnerabilities are both internal, in social, economic, and political terms, and external, as China's neighbors develop increasing qualms about what was supposed to be the peaceful rise of the PRC.

---

[28] Quoted in Flora Lewis, "Foreign Affairs: Japan's Looking Glass," *The New York Times*, November 8, 1989.

[29] The quote and the warnings about rising Japanese influence are from Samuel H. Huntington, "Why International Primacy Matters," *International Security*, Vol. 17, No. 4 (Spring 1993): 68–83, at 75–80.

China's Domestic Constraints

Much of the literature and discussion about China treats that country with awe and foresees its inexorable rise not only to economic predominance, but also in the geopolitical realm, and poses the question of whether its emergence will be peaceful. Books and articles on these themes are too numerous to cite, but a good example is Martin Jacques's *When China Rules the World*. Jacques warns that China is modernizing but not Westernizing, and sees the PRC becoming globally dominant not merely economically, but politically and culturally.[30] In the same vein, billionaire George Soros has claimed, "There is a really remarkable shift of power and influence from the United States to China.... Today China has ... a better functioning government than the United States."[31] Then there are the widely read columns in *The New York Times* by Pulitzer Prize-winning author Thomas Friedman. He marvels at the efficiency of China's government in carrying out future-oriented projects including "space-age" buildings, fast trains, and modern train stations where "all the escalators actually work," while lamenting the lethargy, lack of focus, and inability to get things done in the American system.[32]

While China has often been the subject of uncritical observation, in reality the country faces a host of serious problems that it will need to overcome and for which the solutions are difficult or highly uncertain. These include the likelihood that the economic model of export-led growth cannot be sustained indefinitely. Here, limits to the purchasing power of China's customers – whether in the United States, Asia, or Europe – are likely to be a factor, as are widening resentments over China's predatory and mercantilist behavior. Additional problems include increasing raw material costs, demands for higher wages,

---

[30] Martin Jacques, *When China Rules the World: The End of the Western World and the Birth of a New Global Order* (New York: Penguin, 2009).

[31] "Soros: China Has a Better Functioning Government than U.S.," *Passport: A Blog by the Editors of Foreign Policy*, November 16, 2010, http://blog.foreignpolicy.com/posts/2010/11/16/soros_china_has_better_functioning_government_than_us?sms_ss=digg&at_xt=4ce3eco8cef1d7b5,0, accessed December 13, 2010.

[32] For example, Thomas L. Friedman, "Too Many Hamburgers?" *The New York Times*, September 21, 2010. Friedman does, however, write: "Studying China's ability to invest for the future doesn't make me feel that we have the *wrong* system. It makes me feel that we are abusing our *right* system."

and pressures for changes in currency exchange rates despite the PRC's efforts to keep the yuan from rising in value. China's extraordinary growth has taken place with enormous damage to its environment, as evident in severe pollution of the air, groundwater, and food chain. Furthermore, an enormous commercial and residential real estate bubble suggests the potential for future financial disruption. During the coming ten to fifteen years, China also faces a looming demographic problem. Thanks to its one-child policy and a total fertility rate at times as low as 1.5, the number of young people in the 15–24 age group, that is, those entering the workforce, will drop by one-third, while the number of elderly Chinese whom they will be supporting will rise by more than 100 million. As a consequence, during this period, China's population is expected to peak near 1.4 billion and then enter what a leading demographer cites as an era of "prolonged, even indefinite, population decline and a period of accelerated ageing."[33]

Higher education is also a realm in which China's emergence has been widely touted but remains overstated. Despite an enormous expansion of higher education, China does not yet have institutions comparable to the best research universities in the United States, and the problem is exacerbated by widespread questions of quality and academic standards. Columnists and pundits are fond of citing China's achievement in annually graduating 600,000 engineering majors, compared with a mere 70,000 in America. Nevertheless, half of China's graduates have only associate degrees, and a widely cited 2005 report by the McKinsey Global Institute finds that a mere 10 percent of these Chinese engineers are "employable," as contrasted with 81 percent of the American graduates.[34] Moreover, as China has ramped up higher education, hundreds of thousands of recent college graduates are unable to find jobs that meet their expectations – or for many, any employment for which higher education would have prepared them.[35]

Another illustration of misleading comparisons can be found in a widely publicized study of international test scores for 15-year-old

[33] Wang Fen, "China's Population Destiny: The Looming Crisis," *Current History* (September 2010): 244–251, at 251.

[34] Minxin Pei, "Think Again: Asia's Rise, *Foreign Policy* (July/August 2009): 33–36.

[35] Andrew Jacobs, "China's Army of Graduates Struggles for Jobs," *The New York Times*, December 11, 2010.

students in reading, math, and science. The Program for International Student Assessment (PISA) report, issued in December 2010 by the Organization for Economic Cooperation and Development (OECD), ranked students from Shanghai number one in all three fields. By contrast, the United States ranked seventeenth in reading, thirty-first in math, and twenty-third in sciences. The results triggered an outpouring of laments about America's performance.[36] What was missing from most of these alarms was any recognition that the U.S. results were based on a random selection of 165 public and private schools from the entire country, whereas the Chinese data were based on its richest, most modern, and most developed city, rather than on China as a whole, where the majority of the population remains rural and with a far lower standard of living and education. A more valid comparison would have been to America's most prosperous cities and its best performing school systems such as those in Fairfax, Virginia; Bethesda, Maryland; Highland Park, Illinois; or Beverly Hills, California.

One element missing from most accounts relates to test score validity. A critic of reactions to the PISA results argues that if results for immigrants and those with at least one foreign-born parent (numbers of whom may not yet have acquired English language fluency) are set aside, American students actually outperform Western Europeans and tie with Asians.[37] Another limitation in drawing conclusions about the PISA test results concerns the possibility of corruption and cheating. These remain endemic problems in China, and are not unknown in its educational system. (Indeed, instances of cheating on secondary school test scores have occurred in some U.S. systems.[38]) Thus there is no way of ensuring that the test results, even from Shanghai, accurately portray student achievement.

---

[36] See, e.g., "U.S. Students in Middle of Global Pack: Gauged against Others, Nation Has Little to Show for School Reform Efforts," *The Washington Post*, December 7, 2010, p. A4. To its credit, although only in the eleventh paragraph of the story, *The Post* cautioned that the Shanghai and Hong Kong results should not be interpreted as representative of China as a whole.

[37] Tino Sanandaji, "The Amazing Truth about PISA Scores," *Newgeography.com*, December 28, 2010, http://www.newgeography.com/content/001955-the-amazing-truth-about-pisa-scores-usa-beats-western-europe-ties-with-asia, accessed July 8, 2011.

[38] Paul Gast, "Cheating Scandal Brings Preliminary Reforms to Atlanta Schools," CNN.com, April 8, 2011, http://www.cnn.com/2011/US/07/07/georgia.schools.cheating/index.html, accessed July 8, 2011.

A knowledgeable critic of China, Gordon G. Chang, offers a litany of reasons why the dominant narrative of China becoming the pre-eminent power in the international system within a few short decades should be met with skepticism:

> In addition to its outdated economic model, China faces a number of other problems, including banks with unacknowledged bad loans on their books, trade friction arising from mercantilist policies, a pandemic of defective products and poisonous foods, a grossly underfunded and inadequate social security system, a society that is rapidly aging as a result of the brutally enforced one-child policy, a rising tide of violent crime, a monumental environmental crisis, ever-worsening corruption, and failing schools and other social services. These are just the most important difficulties.[39]

And, finally, there remains the question of whether the political model of authoritarian rule by the Communist Party can be sustained, especially as China's population becomes more educated and increases its access to independent sources of information. An economic crisis could trigger serious political unrest, and the legitimacy of Communist Party rule could be shaken. In the 1990s, the Falun Gong movement, based on a nonviolent combination of graceful physical exercises and peaceful protest, gained some 70 million adherents around the country (a figure larger than the 65 million membership of the Communist Party at that time). In reaction, the regime took draconian steps against the movement, with intensive spying, forceful suppression of its protests, and arrests and killings of its leaders. Although the Falun Gong has been largely suppressed, public resentment over government and police abuses, land seizures, local corruption, and abusive labor practices is growing. According to official Chinese sources, there were 80,000 "mass incidents" in 2007, and unofficial figures indicate that the number may have risen to as many as 127,000 in 2010.[40] As

---

[39] Gordon G. Chang. "The Party's Over: China's Endgame," *World Affairs*, March/April 2010: 61–70.

[40] The 2007 figure came from the Chinese Academy of Social Sciences. The estimate of 127,000 disturbances has been reported variously for 2008 and 2010. See Jeremy Page, "Wave of Unrest Rocks China," *The Wall Street Journal*, June 14, 2011; and Michael Wines, "Vendors' Dispute in China Escalates Into Violent Melee," *The New York Times*, June 13, 2011. *The Economist* cites mostly rural protests, albeit noting that urban unrest is increasing, as with riots by factory workers in Guangdong province. See "Rising power, anxious state," June 25, 2011, p. 14.

Francis Fukuyama has recently noted, in contrasting China with the United States, the Chinese political system has no way of holding its rulers to account, adding, "If I had to bet on these two systems, I'd bet on ours."[41]

China and Its Neighbors

For much of the past decade, China had seemed to emphasize what it termed a strategy of "peaceful rise." The idea was described by then Chinese premier Wen Jiabao in a speech at Harvard in December 2003. Among the salient points of this strategy were claims that China's development depended on and would contribute to world peace, in the future its economic progress would rely more on the domestic market and resources, and China would not seek world hegemony or threaten other countries.[42] In the following years, Beijing set about negotiating and resolving a range of border and maritime issues with many of its neighbors. More recently, however, China's growing economic might, coupled with its rapidly expanding sea power, its expanding and intrusive maritime claims in the East China, South China, and Yellow Seas, and an increasingly confrontational diplomatic posture have intensified anxieties among its East- and South-Asian neighbors. As a result, they have looked toward the United States for reassurance and deterrence. This enhanced attention to regional balance is not entirely new, and at a time when U.S. power has been called into question elsewhere, a number of key Asian powers have actually tightened their bonds with Washington.

The Philippines, for example, which had ousted the United States from its longtime air and naval bases as long ago as 1992, has reacted by welcoming an American naval visit and increased military cooperation. Vietnam, Indonesia, Singapore, and Malaysia, as well as India, in varying degrees, have inclined more toward than away from America. India as early as June 2005 signed a ten-year defense pact with Washington ("New Framework of the US–India Defense Relationship"). In 2008, it successfully concluded a historic agreement on nuclear

[41] Quoted in Nicholas Wade, "From 'End of History' Author, a Look at the Beginning and Middle," *The New York Times*, March 8, 2011.

[42] See, e.g., Zheng Bijian, "China's 'Peaceful Rise' to Great Power Status," *Foreign Affairs*, Vol. 84, No. 5 (September/October, 2005): 18–24.

technology, and in November 2010, it demonstratively welcomed President Obama with an elaborate state visit.

Japan, after a period in which an inexperienced government of the Democratic Party of Japan (DPJ) gained power for the first time and seemed to distance itself from the United States, seemed to reverse course, too, and moved to strengthen this long-standing security relationship and to recast its own defense planning. The motivation was not hard to detect, as Tokyo reacted to Chinese muscle flexing, not only in trade, but also in confrontations over the East China Sea and the Japanese-controlled Senkaku Islands (known as the Diaoyu in Chinese). Tokyo's December 2010 National Defense Program Guidelines referred explicitly to China's military as a "matter of concern for the region" and committed Japan to increasing submarine and mobile forces capable of defending the southern islands. The statement also urged closer military cooperation not only with the United States, but with South Korea, Australia, and India.[43]

A September 2010 incident exemplified Beijing's distinctly more confrontational posture. The encounter began when a Chinese fishing vessel rammed a pair of Japanese coast guard boats near the Senkakus. After the Japanese detained the ship captain, China mounted a virulent campaign against Japan and at one point curtailed shipments of rare earth materials important for Japanese electronics manufacturers. In addition to its tenuous claim to sovereignty over these rocky outcroppings, China has extended its claims in the East China Sea to cover an exclusive economic zone extending close to Japan. It also has made expansive claims about the waters of the South China Sea as a vital national interest comparable to the priority it accords to the Taiwan issue, even though in doing so it encroaches on the continental shelves of a half dozen of its neighbors.[44]

China's problematic behavior also includes its support for states that pose significant problems for the United States and its allies. For example, China has refused to support effective measures against Iran's nuclear program or Sudan's depredations in Darfur. In addition,

---

[43] Martin Fackler, "Japan Announces Defense Policy to Counter China," *The New York Times*, December 16, 2010.

[44] For an informed account of the fishing boat incident and China's claims in the East China and South China Seas, see Gordon G. Chang, "Fishing in Troubled Waters: China's Military Provocations," *The Weekly Standard*, October 11, 2011.

although Beijing has far more leverage over North Korea than any other country, it has been unwilling to rein in the Pyongyang regime, despite the latter's repeated violations of international agreements, its expanding nuclear proliferation program, its aggressive actions against South Korea (the sinking of a patrol boat and directing artillery fire against a South Korean island), and its dangerous exports of nuclear technology and materials.

China's ambitious nuclear missile program has attracted relatively little external attention, even though its previously modest shorter-range and strategic systems are rapidly expanding beyond any concept of minimal deterrence. The PRC's Second Artillery Division (the unit responsible for the strategic missile forces) has reportedly constructed 3,000 miles of underground tunnels in northern China for the concealment and transport of missiles and nuclear warheads. For its domestic audience Beijing describes these facilities as its "Underground Great Wall," and has shown the tunnels on its CCTV television network. In addition, with the development of its DF-31A missiles, China is increasingly capable of striking large areas of the continental United States.[45]

As a consequence of China's increasing assertiveness, the American response becomes critical. Throughout the past half-century, the U.S. presence in East Asia has underpinned stability there. Although there has been no equivalent of an Asian NATO, most of the regional security relationships with Washington have been on a bilateral basis. These have been both formal, as with Japan, South Korea, Taiwan, the Philippines, and Australia, and ad hoc, as with other East- and Southeast-Asian countries. Thus China's neighbors are especially attentive to indications of whether Washington has not only the capacity but also the will to maintain its East-Asian role. American support for Asian allies is seen not so much as confronting China as in

---

[45] For an authoritative analysis of China's nuclear capability, see Robert S. Norris and Hans M. Kristensen, "Chinese Nuclear Forces, 2010," *Bulletin of the Atomic Scientists*, Vol. 66, No. 6 (November/December 2010): 134–141. In addition to being shown on TV, the "Underground Great Wall" has been described in a number of specialized and regional publications, e.g., in the *Ta Kung Pao* daily of Hong Kong, citing the People's Liberation Army's official newsletter, as reported in the *Chosunilbo* (Seoul, South Korea), December 10, 2010, http://english.chosun.com/ site/data/html_dir/2009/12/14/2009121400292.html, accessed December 10, 2010.

deterring it. A case in point is freedom of the seas and insistence on freedom of navigation for American vessels through the East and South China Seas. Conversely, a policy of U.S. disengagement and retrenchment would be more likely to lead to disarray, as countries in the region scramble to mollify Beijing or, as in the case of Japan and South Korea, might instead opt to develop their own nuclear weapons.

Tangible Threats and Shifts in the International Distribution of Power

With the passage of time, the increasing effects of globalization, and the rise of major regional powers, it is no surprise that there have been shifts in the international distribution of power. Although in the recent past it seemed likely that Japan and an increasingly integrated and dynamic European Union would be leading powers well into the twenty-first century, both of them have encountered difficulties that limit their growth and impact. Indeed, the considerably increased share of world GDP now represented by China and other East-Asian countries has come as that of the Europeans and Japanese together has fallen from nearly 40 percent in the early 1970s to somewhere between 25 and 30 percent now.

The United States has experienced a much smaller erosion in its own relative share of world GDP and production, in both cases still maintaining close to the same proportion – about one-fifth, depending on how measured – that it has accounted for since the 1970s. The weaknesses of Europe and Japan have had an effect on American power in the sense that as allies, they have become less capable in terms of economic weight and power projection. This is palpably evident in Europe, where at a time of lagging economic growth, ageing populations, and widening budget deficits, defense budgets have mostly slipped to between 1 and 2 percent of GDP.

In the case of Great Britain, where the financial crisis left an untenable budget deficit of 12 percent of GDP, a newly elected Conservative-Liberal coalition government found itself imposing draconian reductions in the autumn of 2010. This meant slashing domestic spending, cutting the defense budget, and retiring Britain's principal aircraft carrier, the *Ark Royal*, along with its Harrier jump jets. The cuts leave the Royal Navy with only a helicopter carrier and without the ability to deploy strike aircraft until a new carrier is commissioned in 2020. Although Britain remains one of the few European countries to meet the NATO defense-spending target of 2 percent of GDP and has undertaken selective improvements in some areas – for example, its special forces – these cuts seriously reduce its power projection capability.[46] The shortcomings quickly became apparent in Libya, where Britain's role in the intervention was handicapped by the limits on its air and naval forces. One estimate suggests that projected cuts actually will reduce Britain's defense budget between 20 and 30 percent, rather than the official figure of 8 percent.[47]

Meanwhile, and contrary to widely expressed hopes and expectations in the decade following the end of the Cold War, lethal and sustained threats to America's security and vital interests have emerged. These entail several interrelated elements: first, radical Islamist jihadism as an ideology and in its varied organizational forms; second, the enormous dangers posed by nuclear proliferation; third, and closely related, the peril of mass-casualty terrorism, including the risk that non-state actors may eventually acquire and use some form of chemical, biological, radiological, or nuclear weaponry (CBRN).

Newer and unconventional threats such as cyber warfare also have emerged in recent years. While this kind of danger seems esoteric, a full-fledged cyber assault as part of a major conflict with China or Russia, or with a dangerous regional state such as Iran, has the potential to cause major damage to America's electrical grid, oil and gas pipelines, refineries, communications, transportation and computer systems, and the satellite technology essential for civilian and military programs of many kinds.[48]

For the most part, countries antagonistic toward the United States do not pose immediate threats, but their challenge is more indirect

---

[46] "A Retreat, but Not a Rout," *The Economist*, October 21, 2010; and "The Seat of Their Pants," *The Economist*, November 11, 2010.

[47] "The First Casualty," *The Economist*, May 21, 2011.

[48] For knowledgeable treatments of the threat posed by cyber attacks, see Richard A. Clarke and Robert Knake, *Cyber War: The Next Threat to National Security and What to Do About It* (New York: Ecco/HarperCollins, 2010); Jeffrey Carr, *Inside Cyberwarfare: Mapping the Cyber Underworld* (New York: O'Reilly Media, 2010); and Ellen Nakashima, "U.S. Cyber-Spying Report Points to China, Russia," *Washington Post*, November 4, 2011.

and long-term. In the cases of North Korea and Iran, and to a lesser extent Syria and Venezuela, they constitute dangers to regional stability and U.S. interests. While state and non-state adversaries are rarely in a position to confront the United States directly in terms of overt military power, they can pose potential threats.

For the United States, the September 11, 2001 terrorist attacks on New York and Washington were a watershed event, but the peril had been developing during the course of the 1990s. For example, a 1995 plot, the abortive Bojinka Plan, would have destroyed as many as a dozen wide-body passenger aircraft over the Pacific.[49] Even earlier, a September 1993 truck bomb attack on the World Trade Center in New York only narrowly failed in its aim. Had it succeeded, it would have brought down the North Tower, possibly collapsing it against its twin tower at a time of day when both buildings were fully occupied and wreaking a casualty toll substantially greater than that on 9/11.

Abroad, particularly in parts of Europe, there has been a tendency to view 9/11 and radical jihadism through the lenses of earlier and more familiar experiences with violent domestic groups such as the Baader-Meinhof in Germany, the Red Brigades in Italy, the IRA in Northern Ireland, and the Basque separatist ETA in Spain, and to imagine that the danger can be treated primarily as a criminal matter best dealt with by domestic security, policing, and courts. However, the scale of threat cannot be understood in such limited terms, and during the past decade, European governments have become increasingly aware of the danger. For example, the head of Britain's MI5 revealed in November 2006 that as many as 30 "mass casualty" terrorist plots had been identified and that British security services and police were monitoring 200 groups or networks totaling more than 1,600 persons "actively engaged in plotting or facilitating terrorist attacks."[50] Subsequently, in June 2007, there were failed bomb attacks in central London and at

---

[49] See Phillip A. Karber, "Re-Constructing Global Aviation in the Era of the Civilian Aircraft as a Weapon of Destruction," *Harvard Journal of Law and Public Policy*, Vol. 25, No. 2, (Spring 2003): 789; and *Report of the Joint Inquiry into the Terrorist Attacks of September 11, 2001* (Washington, DC: 107th Congress, 2nd Session, House Permanent Select Committee on Intelligence, H. Rept. no. 107–792, and the Senate Select Committee on Intelligence, S. Rept. no. 107–351, December 2002), pp. 129, 192.

[50] Dame Eliza Manningham-Butler, cited in Lee Glendinning, "MI5 head warns of up to 30 terror plots at work in Britain," *The Independent*, November 10, 2006.

Glasgow airport, and in September of that year German police seized three Islamist terrorists planning massive bombings against targets in Germany.[51]

In December 2010, a suicide bomber's attack in Stockholm only narrowly failed to cause numerous casualties among Swedish holiday shoppers when his explosives detonated prematurely. The martyrdom statement of the bomber, Taimour Abdulwahab al-Abdaly, a Swedish citizen of Iraqi origin who had been radicalized while studying in the United Kingdom, promised to kill "your children, daughters, brothers and sisters." Al-Abdaly, who referred to having traveled to the Middle East for "Jihad," denounced his adopted country's "war against Islam," its supporting role in Afghanistan, and its toleration of the Swedish artist Lars Vilks, who in 2007 had drawn caricatures of the Prophet Muhammad and had been condemned by al-Qaeda, which called for him to be "slaughtered like a lamb."[52] The al-Abdaly case, as with a the failures of the Christmas 2009 "underwear" bomber and the May 2010 Times Square bomber, exemplifies the way in which shared extreme ideological beliefs and links among radical jihadist groups transcend national boundaries.

Nuclear terrorism remains the ultimate threat, and no less a figure than the late Osama bin Laden, who had been preaching war against the United States since at least 1996, asserted that acquisition of nuclear weapons was a sacred duty and that al-Qaeda would be justified in killing four million Americans, half of them children. In recognition of this and the wider peril, the bipartisan 9/11 Commission stated in its unanimous report: "The catastrophic threat at this moment in history is more specific. It is the threat posed by *Islamist* terrorism – especially the al Qaeda network, its affiliates, and its ideology."[53]

---

[51] See Kevin Sullivan and Craig Whitlock, "Foreign Doctors Queried in Bomb Plot," *The Washington Post*, July 3, 2007; and Matthias Gebauer and Yassin Musharbash, "More Deadly Than London or Madrid: Islamist Terrorists Planned Massive Attacks in Germany," Spiegel Online, September 5, 2007, http://www.spiegel.de/international/germany/0,1518,504037,00.html, accessed September 11, 2007.

[52] For a detailed account, see Raymond Ibrahim, "Swedish Jihad Revelations," *Middle East Forum*, December 20, 2010, http://www.meforum.org/2811/swedish-jihad-revelations, accessed December 21, 2010.

[53] *The 9/11 Commission Report: Final Report of the National Commission on Terrorist Attacks Upon the United States* (New York: W.W. Norton, 2004), p. 362; italics in original.

Ayman al-Zawahiri, Bin Laden's successor, shares a similar commitment to the nuclear and WMD threat.[54]

It also has been the judgment of prominent and largely nonpartisan authorities on terrorism and proliferation that the use of CBRN may well occur within the next decade. For example, Richard Garwin, a preeminent nuclear scientist and a designer of the hydrogen bomb, testified to Congress that he estimated a "20 percent per year probability [of a nuclear explosion – not just a contaminated, dirty bomb, but a nuclear explosion] with American cities and European cities included."[55] Robert Gallucci, a former senior official and nuclear negotiator in both Democratic and Republican administrations, later Dean of the Georgetown School of Foreign Service and President of the MacArthur Foundation, has written: "[U]nless many changes are made, it is more likely than not that al Qaeda or one of its affiliates will detonate a nuclear weapon in a US city within the next five to ten years."[56] In addition, a survey of one hundred foreign policy experts by *Foreign Policy* magazine and the Center for American Progress found that more than 80 percent expected a terrorist attack on the scale of 9/11 within a decade.[57] Similarly, there were the responses of eighty-five national security and nonproliferation experts to a survey conducted by the U.S. Senate Foreign Relations Committee staff for its then-chairman, Senator Richard Lugar of Indiana. They were asked to predict the likelihood of a CBRN attack occurring anywhere in the world within the following ten years. Their average probability estimate was 29 percent for a nuclear attack, 40 percent for a radiological attack, and 70 percent for some kind of CBRN event.[58]

---

54 Al-Zawahiri's book justifies a potential attack that could kill 10 million Americans. See Rolf Mowatt-Larssen, "Al Qaeda's Nuclear Ambitions," *foreignpolicy.com*, November 16, 2010, http://www.foreignpolicy.com/articles/2010/11/16/al_qaedas_nuclear_ambitions?page=0,1&hidecomments=yes, accessed July 9, 2011.
55 Garwin's testimony took place in March 2007. Quoted in Graham Allison, "Apocalypse When?" *The National Interest* (November/December 2007), p. 13.
56 Robert L. Gallucci, "Avoiding Nuclear Catastrophe: Contemplating Extreme Responses to U.S. Vulnerability," *The ANNALS of the American Academy of Political and Social Science*, No. 607 (September 2006): 51–58, at 52.
57 "The Terrorism Index," *Foreign Policy* 162 (September/October 2007): 62.
58 Lugar Survey on Nuclear Proliferation, June 2005, text at: http://lugar.senate.gov/reports/NPSurvey.pdf

Another reason for concluding that the threat is deep-seated and long-term has to do with the fundamental sources of radical Islamism. Those who downplay the danger argue that the most important causes stem from provocations by America, Israel, or the West, particularly the Afghanistan and Iraq wars, American presence in the Middle East, the Israeli-Palestinian conflict, and the affront caused by the "occupation" of Arab or Muslim lands.[59] But such interpretations do not take sufficiently into account the far deeper origins of radical Islam, and they also oversimply the explanation of contemporary conflicts. In contrast, Assaf Moghadam has provided a compelling refutation of the idea that suicide terrorism is primarily motivated by a resistance to "occupation." Instead he emphasizes the way in which it has evolved into a "globalization of martyrdom."[60]

The fundamental causes of radical jihadism and its manifestations of apocalyptic nihilism lie, to a great extent, in the failure to cope successfully with the disruptions brought by modernity and globalization and in the humiliation experienced, especially by parts of the Arab Muslim world, over the past four centuries. These reactions have been expressed at both individual and societal levels. For example, in an implied reference to the collapse of the Ottoman Empire and thus the end of the Muslim caliphate, which had extended back some thirteen centuries to the time of the Prophet Muhammad, Osama bin Laden's October 2001 video invoked eighty years of Muslim "humiliation" and "degradation" at the hands of the West.[61] The historic reference here is not to the United States (with no colonial history in the region), let alone Israel (which achieved statehood only in

---

[59] Cf. the interpretation of Robert Pape, *Dying to Win: The Strategic Logic of Suicide Terrorism* (New York: Random, 2005); and Robert Pape and James K. Feldman, *Cutting the Fuse: The Explosion of Global Suicide Terrorism and How to Stop It* (Chicago: University of Chicago Press, 2010).

[60] Assaf Moghadam, "Suicide Terrorism, Occupation, and the Globalization of Martyrdom: A Critique of Dying to Win," *Studies in Conflict and Terrorism*, Vol. 29, No. 8 (December 2006): 707-729; and *The Globalization of Martyrdom: Al Qaeda, Salafi Jihad, and the Diffusion of Suicide Attacks* (Baltimore: Johns Hopkins University Press, 2008). Also, e.g., see Michael Scott Doran, "Somebody Else's Civil War," *Foreign Affairs* (January/February 2002): 22–42.

[61] Text of Bin Laden Remarks. "Hypocrisy Rears Its Ugly Head," as broadcast by Al Jazeera television on October 7, 2001; *The Washington Post*, October 8, 2001.

1948), but to the demise of the Ottoman Empire in 1921 and soon afterward the final end of the caliphate, the combined temporal and spiritual authority that had persisted in some form since the seventh century.

Insight into the roots of this problem can be found in the 2002 UN Arab Human Development Report and its subsequent editions. Written by a team of Arab economists for the UN Human Development Report, this study described the contemporary Arab world as afflicted by profound deficits in freedom, in the empowerment of women, and in the diffusion of knowledge and information. The multiple failures of many of these societies to adapt to the challenges of modernity and to meet the needs of their peoples are amplified in the experiences and actions of those individuals who detach themselves from the world they have known but, after coming to the West, are unable to integrate fully into the modern world.[62] Cases in point include the heads of al-Qaeda and the organizers and leaders of the 9/11 attack. These were not the poor and downtrodden, but mostly educated professionals, especially engineers.[63]

It is noteworthy too that the 9/11 attacks took place before the U.S.-led invasion of Iraq and that terrorist strikes against American targets abroad were carried out in 1990s, at a time when the Israeli-Arab peace process seemed to be making real progress. Suicide terrorism elsewhere has had little to do with "occupation" by the West or the Israeli-Palestinian conflict. Attacks in Amman, Bali, Casablanca, Istanbul, Jakarta, and Mumbai, the murder of Dutch filmmaker Theo Van Gogh, the effort to blow up the Indian parliament, the destruction of the dome of the Shiite Golden Mosque in Samarra, deadly Sunni-Shiite violence in Iraq, mass-casualty attacks on public transportation in London and trains in Madrid, the failed Times Square and "underwear" bombings, the unsuccessful suicide bombing in Stockholm, and

---

[62] See especially Bernard Lewis, *What Went Wrong? Western Impact and Middle Eastern Response* (New York: Oxford University Press, 2002); Fouad Ajami, *The Foreigner's Gift: The Americans, the Arabs, and the Iraqis in Iraq* (New York: Free Press, 2006); Laurent Murawiec, *The Mind of Jihad* (New York: Cambridge University Press, 2008).

[63] See, for example, David Berreby, "Engineering Terror: Why Are So Many Extremists from a Single Profession?" *The New York Times Magazine*, September 12, 2010.

numerous other interrupted plots are among multiple indications not only of the wider threat posed by radical jihadism, but also of a deep-seated and fundamental rage against modernity and those identified with it. In analyzing this phenomenon, University of Maryland historian Jeffrey Herf identifies a phenomenon from the interwar era of the past century, which he describes as "reactionary modernism" – that is, the idea held by Nazi ideologists that Germany could utilize modern technology while at the same time rejecting the values of political modernity from the Enlightenment and Western liberalism. Herf identifies parallels between radical Islamists and this ideology of European fascism.[64]

In addition to radical Islamist ideology and terrorism, the proliferation of nuclear weapons is likely to become a profoundly dangerous source of instability and conflict. Over the longer term, and because of the spread of missile technology, the United States will be more exposed to this danger. Not only is there a serious risk that the technology, materials, or weapons themselves will be diverted into the hands of terrorist groups willing to pay almost any price to acquire them, but also that the spread of these weapons carries with it the possibility of devastating regional conflicts.

In assessing nuclear proliferation risks in the late Saddam Hussein's Iraq, in North Korea, and in Iran, some have asserted that deterrence and containment, which seemed to work during the Cold War, will be sufficient to protect the national interests of the United States and those of close allies.[65] Such views are altogether too complacent. The U.S.-Soviet nuclear balance took two decades to become relatively stable, and on at least one occasion – the Cuban Missile Crisis of October 1962 – the parties came to the nuclear brink. Moreover, stable deterrence necessitates assured second-strike capability as well as the knowledge that whichever side suffers an initial nuclear attack would have the capacity to retaliate by inflicting unacceptable damage

---

[64] See *Reactionary Modernism: Technology, Culture, and Politics in Weimar and the Third Reich* (New York: Cambridge University Press, 1994); and "Historic Transgressions: The Uses and Abuses of German History," *International Politik* (Berlin), Transatlantic Edition, Vol. 7 (Spring 2006): 47–53, at 48–49.

[65] Cf. Ian Shapiro, *Containment: Rebuilding a Strategy against Global Terror* (Princeton, NJ: Princeton University Press, 2007); also John Mearsheimer and Stephen Walt, "An Unnecessary War," *Foreign Policy* 134 (January/February 2003): 50–59.

upon the attacker. Importantly, it also requires that one's adversary be a value-maximizing rational actor and be perceived as such. However, with radical Islamic leaders such as those of al-Qaeda or Iran's President Ahmadinejad, there can be no assurance that this is the case.

A robust nuclear balance is difficult to achieve, and in the process of developing a nuclear arsenal, a country embroiled in an intense regional crisis could become the target of a disarming first strike or, on the other hand, may perceive itself to be in a use-it-or-lose-it situation. Moreover, even if America's territory may not be at immediate risk, its interests, bases, and allies surely might be. Careful decision-making control by rational actors in new or pending members of the nuclear club is by no means a foregone conclusion. Illustratively, Saddam Hussein showed himself to be reckless and prone to reject outside information that differed from what he wished to hear.[66] And President Ahmadinejad has expressed beliefs that suggest an erratic grip on reality and that call into question his judgment. For example, he has embraced conspiracy theories about 9/11, fostered Holocaust denial, and called for Israel to be wiped off the map.

The implications of a nuclear-armed Iran go well beyond the risks of an Iranian-Israeli conflict. Once Iran becomes a nuclear power, the Middle East is at risk of entering a fast-moving process of nuclear proliferation. Until now, most Arab governments have not made an effort to match Israel's nuclear arsenal. However, they perceive Iran's nuclear weapons as a strategic threat. For example, in confidential documents released by WikiLeaks, King Abdullah of Saudi Arabia, according to a diplomatic cable, "frequently exhorted the US to attack Iran to put an end to its nuclear weapons programme." The Saudi ambassador to Washington, reporting on King Abdullah's April 2008 meeting with General David Petraeus, wrote, "He told you [Americans] to

---

[66] After the fall of Baghdad in April 2003, the U.S. Joint Forces Command (USJFCOM) undertook a study of the inner workings of Saddam Hussein's regime based on interviews with captured senior Iraqi military and political leaders and official Iraqi documents. For its key findings, see Kevin Woods, James Lacey, and Williamson Murray, "Saddam's Delusions: The View from the Inside," *Foreign Affairs*, Vol. 85, No. 3 (May/June 2006): 2–26. For the full report, see *Iraqi Perspectives Project: A View of Operation Iraqi Freedom from Saddam's Senior Leadership*, available at http://www.foreignaffairs.org/special/iraq/ipp.pdf

cut off the head of the snake."[67] In addition, Jordanian officials called for the Iranian program to be stopped by any means necessary, and leaders of Egypt and the United Arab Emirates were quoted referring to Iran as "evil," and an "existential threat."[68]

A Middle East where more and more states have nuclear arms, a scenario known to experts as a saturated multiplayer environment, would pose an almost insurmountable challenge for deterrence calculations by regional or external powers and a still greater risk of dangerous instability. Contrary to the wishful thinking of some analysts that the possession of nuclear weapons could make Iran more cautious, a nuclear Iran will likely be emboldened, and could press Hezbollah to be more aggressive in Lebanon, flex its muscles in the Persian Gulf, and step up its challenges to U.S. forces in the region.[69]

Here again, the role of China becomes critical. For years, the nuclear and missile programs of North Korea and Iran have been the focus of American and international concern. Yet China has played a unique role in providing technology and equipment to the nuclear proliferation programs of both countries. For example, in late 2010, North Korea gave a tour of its new, state-of-the-art uranium enrichment facility to a leading American nuclear scientist. In all likelihood, the facility could not have been developed by the North Koreans themselves and would have had to depend on technology from another country's program. While Pakistan and Iran could have been the source, in both cases, the technologies they use were derivative of the Chinese program. Moreover, Pakistan's A. Q. Kahn network appears to have been shut down for some years, and Iran has had serious difficulties with its own centrifuge program. Thus a Chinese role is all the more likely,

---

[67] Ian Black and Simon Tisdall, "Saudi Arabia urges US attack on Iran to stop nuclear programme," *The Guardian* (London), Sunday 28 November 2010, http://www.guardian.co.uk/world/2010/nov/28/us-embassy-cables-saudis-iran, accessed December 21, 2010.

[68] These and related statements were extensively reported in *The Guardian*, *The New York Times*, and *Der Spiegel* as well as on the controversial WikiLeaks Web site. See http://www.guardian.co.uk/world/us-embassy-cables-documents/240364, http://www.msnbc.msn.com/id/40405218/ns/world_news-the_new_york_times/, and http://cablegate.wikileaks.org/

[69] Robert J. Lieber and Amatzia Baram, "Containment Breach," *Foreignpolicy.com*, December 22, 2010, http://www.foreignpolicy.com/articles/2009/12/22/containment_breach?page=full

whether carried out with official government support, by a branch of the Chinese military, or by a Chinese firm acting with at least tacit official knowledge.[70]

The PRC at one time also played a significant role in the development of Iran's nuclear program. Even if China no longer is active in supplying technology or materials to Iran's nuclear facilities, it has become Iran's leading trade partner in oil and natural gas, and its leading foreign investor. China's involvement with North Korea is also critical here because of North Korea's close connection with Iran's program.

Twenty-First-Century Realities

The hopes of the post–Cold War era for a benign new world order do not fit the realities of the twenty-first century. The international environment in which the United States finds itself is one in which there are both stubborn and lethal threats. Proliferation, terrorism, radical Islamism, weapons of mass destruction, hostile regional powers, and cyber war are the most serious, though by no means the exclusive, dangers to the United States, its national security, and its vital interests. Cooperation and burden sharing with allies remains important, but the capabilities of America's long-standing alliance partners have eroded. In turn, emerging democracies and regional powers such as Brazil, India, Turkey, Indonesia, and South Africa cannot be relied on to cooperate with the United States in the way that Western Europe and Japan did for half a century.

Multilateral and international mechanisms for responding to these perils can at times be effective, but they are difficult to achieve and often deeply flawed. As an example, consider the efforts of the UN Security Council to halt Iran's nuclear weapons program. Over several years, the Council has passed four sanctions resolutions. These and measures implemented by the United States and some of its allies have imposed significant economic costs on the Iranian regime.

---

[70] The American allowed to visit the facility was the former director of the Los Alamos nuclear laboratory, Siegfried Hecker. See, e.g., Bret Stephens, "China Joins the Axis of Evil: Pyongyang's Nuclear Program Would Have Been Impossible without Beijing," *The Wall Street Journal*, December 7, 2010.

However, the sanctions are incomplete and have significant loopholes. As Western and Japanese businesses and investors have withdrawn from the critical energy sector, Chinese firms have stepped in to invest and develop these resources and to take over export markets abandoned by others. In any case, Teheran shows no signs of yielding to the international community.

Specialized institutions also face serious limitations in their efforts to enforce international rules. The International Atomic Energy Agency (IAEA) has the responsibility for verifying the peaceful use of nuclear technology and possesses a capable technical staff. Yet its effectiveness is limited by dependence on member-state cooperation and as a result it has often failed to detect some of the most egregious covert efforts. Among these have been nuclear proliferation programs by Syria and Libya, as well as Iran's hidden uranium enrichment plant at Natanz and another near Qom.[71]

As an even more telling illustration, consider the attempts to counter North Korea's extensive role in the export of sensitive nuclear technologies and equipment. A much touted UN Security Council Resolution 1874, adopted unanimously June 12, 2009, condemned "in the strongest terms" North Korea's nuclear test of May 25, 2009, tightened sanctions against Pyongyang's nuclear, missile, and proliferation activities, and called on member states to inspect and destroy all banned cargo to and from that country on the high seas or at seaports or airports. They were urged to inspect North Korean ships thought to be carrying banned weapons exports. Yet this resolution, seemingly impressive in its display of the world body's united determination to act, included an almost surreal caveat that halting ships at sea is to be taken "with the consent of the flag state." In other words, a North Korean ship could be stopped only with the agreement of North Korea itself.

The implications of these dangers and of the limits of allied and multilateral cooperation are twofold. First, the international environment is one in which threats to the United States cannot, by and large, be managed by deferring to others. Second, while burden sharing and collaboration with other countries and institutions can be helpful

---

[71] Gregory L. Schulte notes these cases in "Stopping Proliferation Before It Starts," *Foreign Affairs*, Vol. 89, No. 4 (July/August 2010): 85–87.

and even essential, there is no substitute for American engagement and leadership. These realities create a compelling need for the United States to remain actively engaged abroad, and while they do not guarantee that policy makers and the public will continue to support such a role, they provide a powerful motivation to do so, even in the face of constrained resources.

5

Stretch or "Imperial Overstretch"?

"In war, morale is to the material as three is to one."

– Napoleon[1]

Is America overstretched? The question is central to the entire decline debate. After seven decades of global predominance, in World War II, Cold War, post–Cold War, and post-9/11 eras, have the burdens become more than the United States is able – or willing – to bear? As discussed in Chapter 2, the wars in Iraq and Afghanistan, the financial crisis and great recession, an aging population with its costly entitlement programs, and the weight of debt and deficit call into question America's capacity to play its accustomed international role.

This is not only a matter of resources, but also of profound changes in world affairs. Globalization, the rise of China and other emerging powers, popular revolts against long-entrenched Arab despots, erosion in the capability of America's traditional allies, and the dangers posed by terrorism, radical Islamism, nuclear proliferation, and failing or failed states shape a world very different from the one in which the Cold War came to an end little more than two decades ago.

Not surprisingly, there are those who either urge retrenchment as desirable in itself or who foresee that serious cutbacks in America's

---

[1] My idiomatic translation from the French, "*A la guerre, les trois quarts sont des affaires morales, la balance des forces réeles n'est que pour un autre part*," in *The Oxford Dictionary of Quotation* (New York: Oxford University Press, 4th ed., 1992), p. 489n.

foreign commitments will become unavoidable as a result of the costs and burdens America has borne. Among the most widely cited arguments on this point is the idea of imperial overstretch, put forward by Paul Kennedy. His 1987 book, *The Rise and Fall of the Great Powers,*[2] gave prominence to the idea, although the concept can be found at least as far back as Edward Gibbon's classic *History of the Decline and Fall of the Roman Empire*, published in 1776. Kennedy's book gained wide attention at the time it was published, but it appeared just two years before the opening of the Berlin Wall and the subsequent end of the Cold War. These momentous events, together with the collapse of the Soviet Union and America's emergence as the sole superpower, caused Kennedy to pull back from the Cassandra-like warning in his book. The change was conspicuously evident in his 2002 essay contrasting America's predominance with that of other empires over the past 2,000 years, including those of Charlemagne, Rome, Persia, and China, and in which he exulted, "Nothing has ever existed like this disparity of power; nothing."[3] In more recent years, however, Kennedy has returned to his original diagnosis, now describing America as "slowly and naturally losing its abnormal status in the international system and returning to being one of the most prominent players in the small club of great powers," and depicting this in terms of the pattern of rise and decline followed by Great Britain. Although Kennedy acknowledges the United States is a much larger country and one with far more resources than the United Kingdom, he insists that its "long-term trajectory is roughly the same."[4] And he has had plenty of company among scholars, commentators, and political figures.

Among the most thoughtful of those who view the United States as compelled to make serious cuts in its foreign and security commitments is Michael Mandelbaum. He finds this to be the inevitable result of fiscal deficit and debt, although unlike most others who anticipate or prescribe these reductions, he frankly acknowledges the adverse consequences that are likely to result.[5]

[2] Paul Kennedy, *The Rise and fall of the Great Powers: Economic Change and Military Conflict from 1500 to 2000* (New York: Random, 1987).

[3] "The Eagle Has Landed," *Financial Times* (London), February 1, 2002.

[4] Paul Kennedy, "Back to Normalcy: Is America Really in Decline?" *The New Republic*, December 21, 2010.

[5] Michael Mandelbaum, *The Frugal Superpower: America's Global Leadership in a Cash-Strapped Era* (New York: PublicAffairs, 2010).

Other pundits also urge a less ambitious world role for the United States. Richard Haass, president of the Council on Foreign Relations and former head of the State Department's Policy Planning Staff, cites the 1991 Gulf War, which drove Saddam Hussein out of Kuwait, as a war of necessity, contrasted with the 2003 war against Saddam, Operation Iraqi Freedom (OIF), as a war of choice.[6] Yet with rare exceptions, notably Pearl Harbor and the initial post-9/11 action in Afghanistan, such distinctions are almost always less clear-cut, and most wars ultimately are, to a greater or lesser extent, matters of choice. Although Desert Storm benefitted from the international legitimacy bestowed by the historic UN Security Council Resolution 678 and proved to be a noteworthy military success, the course of action embarked on by the administration of George H. W. Bush in 1990–1991 was politically contested early on and became the subject of an intense debate prior to the start of hostilities.

Many scholars – for example, Christopher Layne, Andrew Bacevitch, and various international relations realists – have long argued for strategies of retrenchment, offshore balancing, or something close to outright isolationism, regardless of the consequences.[7] A prominent German foreign policy expert, Eberhard Sandschneider, adds that the task now is one of "Managing the Successful Decline of the West."[8]

From a different vantage point, liberal internationalists also have tended to advocate a less assertive American foreign policy. They have argued that strategies of cooperation and reliance on international institutions afford a means for coping with problems of global order, but with less cost to the United States. Much of this viewpoint was expressed during the years of the George W. Bush administration, in reaction to Iraq and other manifestations of the Bush Doctrine. Ironically, with the coming to office of the Obama administration, some liberal internationalists found themselves cross-pressured in reaction to flagrant human rights abuses in Iran and then the eruption of popular

---

[6] Richard Haass, *War of Necessity, War of Choice: A Memoir of Two Iraq Wars* (New York: Simon & Schuster, 2010).

[7] Andrew Bacevitch, *The Limits of Power: The End of American Exceptionalism* (New York: Metropolitan Books, 2008).

[8] Sandschneider is Director of the Research Institute at the German Council on Foreign Relations. The wording is taken from the title of his talk to the Transatlantic Academy, German Marshall Fund, Washington, DC, February 24, 2011.

revolts that characterized the Arab Spring. As a case in point, Anne-Marie Slaughter, who had headed Policy Planning under Secretary of State Hillary Clinton, responded to the uprising in Libya by decrying the administration's initial passivity and calling for intervention against the Qaddafi regime.[9] According to accounts at the time, Secretary Clinton, UN Ambassador Susan Rice, and foreign policy advisor Samantha Power lobbied President Obama in favor of the use of force.

But are such strategies feasible and does the United States really face a tenacious problem of overstretch from which there is no recourse except to seek relief by means of retrenchment? Previous portions of this book have assessed the economic and financial components of the question. Hence this chapter examines other dimensions, especially military commitments and problems of burden sharing. Although military power is not identical to primacy, it provides a good marker or indicator, especially in assessing stretch or overstretch. The limits of collective action and burden sharing are next examined, both with allies and in relation to the role played by rising powers. The likely consequences, were America ultimately to opt for a strategy of disengagement, need to be considered as well, along with evidence about the public's willingness to support intervention abroad despite ongoing burdens. Here too, material factors are likely to weigh less than matters of political judgment, will, and leadership.

Military Costs and Capabilities

On an annual basis, the United States in fiscal year 2011 allotted $725 billion for defense. The total, including the costs of war in Afghanistan and commitments in Iraq, amounted to 5.1 percent of GDP.[10] In percentage terms, this made up nearly 54 percent of federal discretionary spending.[11] The figure for 2011 represented a post-9/11 peak,

---

[9] Anne-Marie Slaughter, "Fiddling While Libya Burns," *The New York Times*, March 13, 2011.

[10] Unless otherwise noted, defense spending and percentage figures in this chapter are from the Office of Management and Budget, *Historical Tables, Budget of the U.S. Government: Fiscal Year 2012* (Washington, DC: U.S. Government Printing Office, 2011), Tables 8.2–8.4.

[11] Data from Table 5.1 below.

but in anticipation of force reductions in both Iraq and Afghanistan, the Obama administration's defense budget projections provided for substantial cuts in defense spending, so that by 2015 the figure would decline to just 3.6 percent of GDP. Automatic cuts triggered by failure of the congressional "suppercommittee" to agree on deficit reduction could – if eventually implemented – require an additional $600 billion in decreases for the military.

The defense spending numbers involve very large sums of money, but how are we to judge what they represent? A familiar argument from those urging major reductions in the military budget is that such spending vastly exceeds that of other countries and that reductions can be made without jeopardizing national security. For example, in November 2010, after the president's bipartisan Commission on Fiscal Responsibility and Reform suggested defense reductions of as much as $100 billion per year (described by then Secretary of Defense Robert Gates as potentially "disastrous"), the Commission's trial balloon received support from pressure groups that had long advocated defense cutbacks, such as the Project on Defense Alternatives and the Coalition for a Realistic Foreign Policy.[12] For some of those urging cuts of this magnitude, the issue is less a matter of military over-stretch than of competing domestic budget priorities, while for others it is a matter of differing conceptions of America's role in foreign affairs.

The dollar amounts are enormous, yet they represent a relatively modest percentage of GDP in comparison with double-digit amounts during the first two decades of the Cold War and with still significant percentages in the later years. For example, during the Korean War (1950–1953), spending peaked at 14.2 percent of GDP in 1953, and as late as 1959, it remained as high as 10.0 percent. At the height of the Vietnam War in 1968, defense spending as a percentage of GDP amounted to 9.4 percent, and at the peak of the Reagan buildup in 1986, it still totaled 6.2 percent.[13] (See Table 5.1)

---

[12] See "Experts Letter on Defense Spending," signed by forty-six defense policy scholars and practitioners, November 18, 2010, http://www.comw.org/pda/fulltext/NCFRexpertsletter.pdf, accessed February 23, 2011.

[13] Data prior to 1962 from Office of Management and Budget, *Historical Tables, Budget of the United States Government, Fiscal Year 2005* (Washington, DC: GAO, 2004).

TABLE 5.1. *U.S. Military Spending as Percent of GDP and Discretionary Outlays*

Fiscal Year	U.S. Military Spending as Percent of GDP	U.S. Military Spending as Percentage of Discretionary Outlays
1940	1.7	
1941	5.6	
1942	17.8	
1943	37.0	
1944	37.8	
1945	37.5	
1946	19.2	
1947	5.5	
1948	3.5	
1949	4.8	
1950	5.0	
1951	7.4	
1952	13.2	
1953	14.2	
1954	13.1	
1955	10.8	
1956	10.0	
1957	10.1	
1958	10.2	
1959	10.0	
1960	9.3	
1961	9.4	
1962	9.2	72.9
1963	8.9	71.3
1964	8.5	69.5
1965	7.4	65.6
1966	7.7	65.4
1967	8.8	67.6
1968	9.4	69.6
1969	8.7	70.5
1970	8.1	68.1
1971	7.3	64.5
1972	6.7	61.7
1973	5.9	59.1
1974	5.5	58.4
1975	5.5	55.5
1976	5.2	51.2
1977	4.9	49.5
1978	4.7	47.8
1979	4.7	48.7
1980	4.9	48.7

(continued)

TABLE 5.1 *(continued)*

Fiscal Year	U.S. Military Spending as Percent of GDP	U.S. Military Spending as Percentage of Discretionary Outlays
1981	5.2	51.3
1982	5.7	57.0
1983	6.1	59.4
1984	5.9	60.1
1985	6.1	60.9
1986	6.2	62.4
1987	6.1	63.6
1988	5.8	62.6
1989	5.6	62.2
1990	5.2	60.0
1991	4.6	60.0
1992	4.8	56.7
1993	4.4	54.2
1994	4.0	52.1
1995	3.7	50.2
1996	3.4	49.9
1997	3.3	49.7
1998	3.1	49.0
1999	3.0	48.1
2000	3.0	48.0
2001	3.0	47.2
2002	3.3	47.5
2003	3.7	49.1
2004	3.9	50.7
2005	4.0	51.0
2006	3.9	51.1
2007	4.0	52.6
2008	4.3	54.0
2009	4.7	53.1
2010	4.8	51.1
2011 (estimate)	5.1	53.7
2012 (estimate)	4.7	54.5
2013 (estimate)	4.0	53.8
2014 (estimate)	3.7	54.0
2015 (estimate)	3.6	54.5
2016 (estimate)	3.4	54.4

Source: Table 6.1 Composition of Outlays: 1940–2016. "Historical Tables." *Fiscal Year 2012 Budget of the U.S. Government. United States. Office of Management and Budget. Accessed 19 Feb. 2011.* <http://www.whitehouse.gov/omb/budget/Historicals>.

Table 8.7 Outlays for Discretionary Programs: 1962–2016. "Historical Tables." *Fiscal Year 2012 Budget of the U.S. Government. United States. Office of Management and Budget. Accessed 21 March 2011.* <http://www.whitehouse.gov/omb/budget/Historicals>.

TABLE 5.2. *U.S. Military Spending by Decade*

Decade	Average U.S. Military Spending as Percent of GDP	Average U.S. Military Spending as Percent of Discretionary Outlays
1940–1949	17.0	
1950–1959	10.4	
1960–1969	8.7	69.1*
1970–1979	5.9	56.5
1980–1989	5.8	58.8
1990–1999	4.0	53.0
2000–2010	3.9	50.5
2011–2016 (estimate)	4.1	54.2

* Data only available from 1962–1969.
Source: Table 6.1 Composition of Outlays: 1940–2016. "Historical Tables." *Fiscal Year 2012 Budget of the U.S. Government. United States. Office of Management and Budget. Accessed 19 Feb. 2011.* <http://www.whitehouse.gov/omb/budget/Historicals>.

With the end of the Cold War, the administrations of George H. W. Bush and Bill Clinton carried out major reductions in forces and budgets. Consequently, on the eve of the September 11, 2001 terrorist attacks on New York and Washington, spending on the military as a percentage of GDP had dropped to 3.0. These reduced expenditures resulted from cuts of approximately one-third in active duty forces as well as a significant slowing in weapons procurement. The post-9/11 increases, rising to 4.8 percent of GDP in 2010 and 5.1 percent in 2011, reflected the continuing costs of Afghanistan and Iraq, as well as anti-terrorism measures elsewhere and long-standing regional commitments. Even so, at a time when the United States has been involved in two wars, the amounts pale in comparison with expenditures during the Korean and Vietnam conflicts.

Of course, the human costs of war cannot and should not be expressed simply in cold economic statistics. American military casualties in Iraq and Afghanistan have totaled more than 6,200 dead, as well as more than 30,000 wounded. These represent painful losses, even though the toll has been far less than in Korea (37,000 dead) and Vietnam (58,000).

With the winding down of the American military presence in Iraq, the commitment in Afghanistan remains an ongoing subject of debate, both among elites and the public. Nonetheless, the public has, for the most part, remained supportive when asked whether or not the United States made a mistake in sending military forces to Afghanistan. Polling by Gallup throughout the conflict found that supporters outnumbered opponents and sometimes by substantial margins. However, after nearly a decade of war, the successful killing of Bin Laden, and with the burden of paying for the war weighing on the economy, there was increasing sentiment to bring the troops home.[14] President Obama's June 2011 announcement to withdraw the 33,000 surge forces by September 2012 and to remove the remaining troops by the end of 2014 received broad public support. Almost three-fourths of the public favored the plan, although there remained wider disagreement about the timetable.[15]

The pattern of support was consistent with previous evidence on the public's casualty tolerance (as noted in Chapter 3). What determines whether the American people will support a foreign military commitment depends less on the outright number of U.S. casualties than on whether the public regards the war as justifiable, and especially whether the United States can prevail. Thus Christopher Gelpi, Peter Feaver, and Jason Reifler have shown that public tolerance for the human toll of war is mainly affected by beliefs about the likelihood of success and the rightness or wrongness of the war. And in their analysis, expectations about success are what matters most.[16]

During the Vietnam conflict, bitter domestic arguments erupted about the wisdom and justification for the war (which was fought with

---

[14] An August 2011 poll of likely voters found 59% wanting the troops to return home immediately or within a year. See "59% Want Troops Home from Afghanistan," *RasmussenReports.com*, August 11, 2011, http://www.rasmussenreports.com/ public_content/politics/current_events/afghanistan/59_want_troops_home_from_ afghanistan, accessed August 23, 2011.

[15] Seventy-two percent of adults favored the Obama plan. On the withdrawal timetable, 30% agreed, 33% favored faster withdrawal, and 31% opposed setting a timetable. See Lydia Saad, "Americans Broadly Favor Obama's Afghanistan Pullout Plan," *Gallup.com*, June 29, 2011, http://www.gallup.com/poll/148313/Americans-Broadly-Favor-Obama-Afghanistan-Pullout-Plan.aspx, accessed July 11, 2011. On the pattern of sustained support, see Jeffery M. Jones, "Americans Less Pessimistic about U.S. Progress in Afghanistan," November 29, 2010, *Gallup.com*, http://www. gallup.com/poll/144944/Americans-Less-Pessimistic-Progress-Afghanistan.aspx, accessed July 11, 2011.

[16] Christopher Gelpi, Peter Feaver, and Jason Reifler, "Success Matters: Casualty Sensitivity and the War in Iraq," *International Security*, Vol. 30, No. 3 (Winter 2005/2006): 7–46, at 8.

a draftee army rather than a volunteer military). From the autumn of
1968 onward, an increasing majority of the public turned against the
war, creating a climate of opinion in which Congress eventually cut
off funding for American military action in June 1973, and later halted
military assistance to South Vietnam in December 1974. The Vietnam
trauma gave rise to a belief that any future military interventions would
have to be quick, decisive, and without significant U.S. casualties, as
expressed in the adage, "Win quickly or get out."[17] This approach
certainly seems to have influenced administrations of both parties during the remainder of the 1970s and throughout the 1980s, and even
the successful uses of American power in the 1990s, in Desert Storm,
as well as in Bosnia and Kosovo, seemed to reflect these assumptions.
Nonetheless, the ability of the George W. Bush and Obama administrations to act as they did in Iraq and Afghanistan strongly suggests
that the public's casualty tolerance is greater than had been assumed
in the aftermath of Vietnam. As a result, and subject to the conditions
cited by Gelpi, Feaver, and Reifler, this concern should not prevent
the United States from playing a leading role in circumstances where
national leaders make the decision to commit combat troops abroad.

If we are to assess the burden of current military commitments in
terms of casualties as well as in relative economic terms, they seem
manageable when contrasted with the record of the Cold War. Importantly, however, the burden on a significantly smaller active duty
force and its aging weaponry must be taken into account. By some
calculations, the military campaigns in Afghanistan and Iraq were
adversely affected by decisions not to commit greater numbers of
troops. Whether these commitments were constrained by force size
is a matter of debate. As a rule of thumb, for every military unit in
the field, two others must be undergoing periods of resting, refitting,
and retraining. Because of this constraint and in order to cope with
long wars in Afghanistan and Iraq, the Pentagon adopted a series of
special measures. These included the call-ups of Reserve and National
Guard units for training and deployment abroad. It also meant sending

---

[17] A quarter-century ago, William Schneider found that "If a vital national interest is at
stake, Americans want to take action that is swift, decisive, and relatively cost-free."
"'Rambo' and Reality: Having It Both Ways," in Kenneth Oye, Robert J. Lieber, and
Donald Rothchild (eds.), *Eagle Resurgent? The Reagan Era in American Foreign
Policy* (Boston: Little, Brown, 1987), p. 59.

troops for repeated tours of duty, so that many officers and enlisted men found themselves returning to combat assignments on two, three, or more occasions. At times, the Army also resorted to a "stop loss" procedure, in which enlistments were extended involuntarily for short periods of time. In addition, the ranks of both the Army and Marines were buttressed by temporary increases in the active forces.

There is no doubt that these wars and the intense tempo of operations placed a strain on the career military, as reflected in personal stress, marital problems, and increased incidence of post-traumatic stress disorder (PTSD). Despite these pressures, however, the overall performance of American military units remained quite high. While the Army and Marine Corps were stretched, they were not overstretched, let alone "broken," as claimed by some critics. Painfully at times, the military also showed an impressive capacity for learning, as had been the case in other long wars, including World War II and Vietnam. As a result, the country possesses experienced professional forces, skillful in counterinsurgency, and battle-hardened. Although the intense pace of assignment abroad puts pressure on the military and causes some problems in reenlistment, the armed forces have nonetheless been able to maintain sufficient recruitment and retention ratios. But a very different problem causes some of the most talented officers to leave. It involves frustration with bureaucracy and a promotion system that gives insufficient weight to merit rather than time served and the ability to avoid controversy. The 2008 resignation of Lt. Colonel John Nagl, a Rhodes Scholar, brilliant military innovator, and one of the authors, with General David Petraeus, of the Army's important counterinsurgency field manual, provides a case in point.[18] And no less an authority than former Secretary of Defense Robert Gates, in a valedictory address, warned that one of the biggest threats to the Army could come from its "bureaucratic and sometimes rigid culture."[19]

In judging whether American forces are or will be overstretched, the issue of weapons systems importantly comes into play. Considerable attention has been devoted to the costs of modern weapons

---

[18] For an interview with Lt. Colonel Nagl concerning his decision to retire from the military, see Tim Kane, "Why Our Best Officers Are Leaving," *The Atlantic*, January/February 2011, pp. 80–85.

[19] Greg Jaffe, "Gates envisions a new game plan for the Army," *The Washington Post*, February 26, 2011.

and the need to cancel programs that have proved too expensive or that exist more to meet the demands of members of Congress and selected defense contractors than the needs of U.S. troops to prevail in combat. Some redundant or excessively expensive programs have been cancelled, such as a costly alternative engine for the F-35 aircraft program. Others, including an airborne laser and the Defense Department health care system, have been the subjects of protracted budget battles as the Joint Chiefs of Staff and the Secretary of Defense have repeatedly sought to curtail them.

Cost-effectiveness is of critical importance, and there will always be a need to prioritize among weapons systems, because even under the best of circumstances, not all can be funded. Nonetheless, there is reason for concern about aging weapons and delays in modernization. For example, while the electronics and weaponry have been updated and modernized, many bomber aircraft are older than the pilots who fly them, as are the airborne tankers that refuel them.

Another real problem concerns not just quality but numbers of ships and planes. During the past two decades, the U.S. Navy has reduced its fleet from nearly 400 ships to 285, giving it the smallest number since World War I. In turn, production of the most advanced and capable air-superiority fighter plane, the F-22 "Raptor," has been halted, which will leave the United States with a total inventory of just 186 of these aircraft, far fewer than the original target of 750 planes.[20] In addition, projected numbers of the F-35 Joint Strike Fighter, an advanced stealth tactical aircraft for ground attack and air defense, not yet in full production, have been reduced because of mounting costs.

American military technology is likely to ensure that these systems are superior to those of any potential adversary, but numbers matter and, beyond a certain point, quality is an insufficient substitute for quantity. War games and simulations illustrate the problem. In a hypothetical conflict over the Taiwan Strait, even though the United States would maintain a 6-to-1 kill ratio against Chinese aircraft, the Americans have been predicted to lose. Because of numbers and the need to operate from more distant bases in Guam and Okinawa after

---

[20] See Michael Auslin, "Tipping Point in the Indo-Pacific," *The American Interest* (Spring 2010): 24; and "Defense Spending in a Time of Austerity," *The Economist*, August 28, 2010.

airfields in Taiwan were quickly taken out, the Chinese would still have enough surviving combat aircraft to "shred" U.S. tanker aircraft and command, control, and intelligence planes. Similar problems face U.S. Navy aircraft. Although superior in technology and striking power, and even if every missile aimed by American planes at their adversaries found its target, Navy aviation would have difficulty operating in this environment because of the remaining numbers of attackers and the threat of anti-ship missiles to an aircraft carrier battle group.[21] In view of these considerations, further cuts in weapons procurement can compromise the U.S. ability to prevail on the battlefield.

Moreover, asymmetric warfare poses a problem too. Rather than relying simply on matching the United States in modern ships or advanced aircraft, potential adversaries such as China and Iran also focus on anti-aircraft, anti-ship, and anti-satellite missile systems, as well as on cyber warfare, all of which have the potential to neutralize an otherwise potentially overwhelming American advantage.

As a wider illustration of challenges facing the American military, the *National Military Strategy* issued by the Joint Chiefs of Staff sets out an ambitious set of missions for the armed forces, with no reduction in the tasks they are expected to undertake.[22] Although the military services have performed effectively despite the pressures and constraints under which they operate, additional reductions in force size and weapons programs could mean that they will be asked to undertake roles that exceed their capacity to perform or that expose them to much greater dangers and losses.[23]

---

[21] "Tough Odds in a China Battle," posted by David A. Fulghum, *Aviation Week*, December 28, 2010, at http://www.aviationweek.com/aw/blogs/defense/index.jsp?plckController=Blog&plckScript=blogScript&plckElementId=blogDest&plckBlogPage=BlogViewPost&plckPostId=Blog%3a27ec4a53-dcc8-42do-bd3a-01329aef79a7Post%3ab786b890-591a-474d-95ee-00b754d2a188, accessed November 26, 2011.

[22] *National Military Strategy of the United States of America: Redefining America's Military Leadership* (Washington, DC: Chairman of the Joint Chiefs of Staff, February 8, 2011), http://graphics8.nytimes.com/packages/pdf/world/atwar/NMS-110208.pdf, accessed November 26, 2011.

[23] Note the analysis by Max Boot, who criticizes the consensus of recent years, "Let's Do Everything We're Doing Now, but Do It with Fewer People and Less Money." See "Matching Resources to Defense Commitments," http://www.commentarymagazine.com/blogs/boot, accessed February 11, 2011.

Throughout its history, the United States has exhibited a pattern of fighting wars with great tenacity and force, but in the aftermath of war tending to cut back so severely on manpower and capabilities as to jeopardize its capacity to act when it is again faced with foreign dangers that require the use of force. This has been the American experience following the Revolutionary War, the Civil War, World War I, World War II, Korea, Vietnam, and the Persian Gulf War, and with the winding down of wars in Iraq and Afghanistan, there will be strong pressure for deep cuts. To be sure, the extraordinary size of forces and amounts of equipment required during wartime do not need to be maintained at the same levels afterward, but reductions need to be prudent. Past experience suggests that America's adversaries can be emboldened when they perceive that U.S. capability and deterrence are constrained. And even when this is not the case, options for dealing with potential threats can be limited. For example, a one-third cut in military personnel during the decade after the end of the Cold War provided a substantial peace dividend, but left the forces stretched to cope with post-9/11 deployments in Afghanistan and Iraq, where in both cases, larger numbers of troops might have made it possible to avoid or at least diminish the intense and costly insurgencies that followed.[24]

Of course there remains the important question not only of whether the United States can afford existing levels of military expenditure, but whether competing domestic priorities may impose tenacious constraints. From this perspective, the place of defense spending as a proportion of the federal budget (where debt service and entitlements take up a rapidly increasing share) may be as important as the percentage of GDP. According to data from the Office of Management and Budget, military spending as a percentage of discretionary outlays averaged 50.5 percent in the decade from 2000 to 2010 and is estimated at 54.2 percent for the first half of the following decade

---

[24] Max Boot discusses the consequences and provides numbers for the cuts in the armed forces that took place after each conflict: Revolutionary War (from 35,000 to 10,000), Civil War (1 million to 50,000), World War I (2.9 million to 250,000), World War II (12 million to 1.4 million), Vietnam (3.5 million to 2 million), and the Cold War (2.1 million to 1.3 million). See "A Defense Budget Lesson We Never Learn," *The Washington Post*, July 30, 2010.

(2011–2016).[25] This represents a hefty share of discretionary federal spending and thus almost inevitably will become a target for budget reductions. Nonetheless, these percentages are lower than during the Cold War, where as late as the 1980s, defense represented an average of 58.8 percent (see Table 5.1).

Beyond numbers of troops, ships, and planes, and the accounting of dollars and percentages, there are other, more intangible dimensions. The ability to adapt to changing threats and to incorporate advances in technology, weapons, and doctrine is critical.[26] The American lead in applying smart weapons, precision-guided munitions, and drone aircraft has been impressive, as well as in learning (and re-learning) effective counterinsurgency. However, cycles of innovation and the need for adaptation are unlikely ever to end. China's development and deployment of modern weapons, Iran and North Korea's nuclear programs, insurgents' use of ever more sophisticated improvised explosive devices (IEDs), and the growing menace of cyber warfare illustrate the ongoing nature of this military competition.

Finally, there are the vital elements of national will and the signals it sends to both allies and adversaries. During the latter years of the Cold War, British strategist Michael Howard observed how America's deployments in Europe along with its strategic doctrine provided both deterrence of the Soviets and reassurance for the NATO allies.[27] Now, at a time when America's adversaries perceive the United States as wearied by wars, financially weakened, and tempted to turn inward, countries such as China, Iran, and Russia are inclined to test its resolve in East Asia, the Middle East, and elsewhere. Under these conditions, as two thoughtful strategists, A. Wesley Mitchell and Jakub Grygiel,

---

[25] Source: Table 6.1 Composition of Outlays: 1940–2016, and Table 8.7 Outlays for Discretionary Programs: 1962–2016, "Historical Tables," *Fiscal Year 2012 Budget of the U.S. Government*, Office of Management and Budget, http://www.whitehouse. gov/omb/budget/Historicals, accessed February 19, 2011.
       "Historical Tables." *Fiscal Year 2012 Budget of the U.S. Government. United States. Office of Management and Budget*, http://www.whitehouse.gov/omb/budget/ Historicals, accessed March 21, 2011.

[26] The organizational capacity for major military innovations is especially important. See Michael C. Horowitz, *The Diffusion of Military Power: Cause and Consequences for International Politics* (Princeton, NJ: Princeton University Press, 2010), pp. 1–8.

[27] Michael Howard, "Reassurance and Deterrence: Western Defense in the 1980s," *Foreign Affairs* Vol. 61, No. 2 (Winter 1982–1983): 309–324.

note, "Credibility resides not only in capacity but also in constancy of purpose."[28] In sum, although the extant American capabilities, measured in troops, weapons, defense dollars, and ability to project power at great distances, matter greatly, the elements of policy, determination, and willingness to meet its commitments constitute a vital element in any assessment of American power.

Problems of Collective Action: Allies and Burden Sharing

To answer the question of whether the United States has become overstretched requires assessing not only its capabilities, but also those of its closest allies. Those who advocate steep cuts in the U.S. defense budget point not only to spending said to be greater than that of the next dozen or even twenty countries combined, but to the cumulative weight of America's allies. A well-respected defense expert, Michael O'Hanlon of the Brookings Institution, cites the cumulative might of more than sixty countries comprising the U.S. alliance system and representing some 80 percent of global military spending.[29] The argument is plausible, but one problem concerns whether the figures for China (whose military spending is known to widely surpass its official figures) can in any way be accurately calculated. Problems also exist in assessing the defense spending of Iran, Venezuela, Syria, and North Korea. Moreover, much of this analysis is backward looking rather than geared to future trends. For example, Russia has embarked on a major military modernization program that will boost the numbers of its modern nuclear submarines, combat aircraft, helicopters, and warships. As a result, Moscow's spending on defense will triple from 0.5 percent of GDP to 1.5 percent.[30] As for China, its military modernization is continuing at a rapid pace, with budgets increasing by more than 10 percent or more per year.

A more fundamental issue is what the spending actually buys in useable military assets and power projection. For example, Britain

---

[28] A. Wesley Mitchell and Jakub Grygiel, "The Vulnerability of Peripheries," *The American Interest* (March/April 2011): 12.

[29] O'Hanlon is cited at length in "American Military Spending: Threatening a Sacred Cow," *The Economist*, February 12, 2011.

[30] "Russia Plans $650 Billion Defence Spend Up to 2020," BBC News, February 24, 2011, http://www.bbc.co.uk/news/world-europe-12567043, accessed February 24, 2011.

has been America's foremost ally and, despite budget cuts enacted by a coalition Conservative/Liberal government, remains committed to spending at least 2 percent of GDP on defense. The United Kingdom also maintains modern aircraft, ships, nuclear submarines, and special forces. Yet, as noted in Chapter 4, its capacity to project power has been greatly diminished. For more than ninety years, Britain has not only been America's closest ally; it has also deployed large fighting forces in wars where it fought side by side with the United States. Since World War II, the United Kingdom has been a major combatant in Korea (1950–1953), Operation Desert Storm (1991), the war in Afghanistan, and then in Iraq in 2003. But those days are over. The scrapping of the Navy's only active aircraft carrier, *Ark Royal*, together with its Harrier jump jets, leaves Britain without carrier strike capability until the year 2020. With cuts in the size of its army, elimination of more than one-third of its artillery and tanks, and with the ability to commit no more than 7,500 soldiers to a sustained foreign deployment, Britain's capacity to project power as a fighting ally has been greatly diminished.[31] And Britain has been the most capable of America's allies.

Apart from France, which retains some power projection capacity, the record elsewhere in Europe is even more modest. Most of the alliance members fall well below the NATO target of at least 2 percent of GDP to be spent on defense. Among major NATO members, only France is committed to exceed that threshold. But Germany, Europe's most economically powerful and populous country, spends just 1.4 percent and is shrinking its army by up to one-third while ending conscription. The figures for others are no better: Italy 1.3 percent, Spain 1.1 percent, and Canada 1.5 percent. Among those few countries that nearly meet or exceed the 2 percent threshold, Greece is at 2.9 percent and Turkey is at 1.9 percent, but their forces are directed as much against one another (and for Turkey against PKK Kurdish insurgents) as to any shared commitment with the United States.[32]

---

[31] See "The Emperor's Clothes," *The Economist*, March 3, 2011; Michael Birnbaum, "Ú.S., NATO See Risks as Defense Budgets Shrink across Europe," *The Washington Post*, February 15, 2011; Max Boot, "Britain Bows Out of the Security Game," *The Wall Street Journal*, October 21, 2010; "The Seat of Their Pants," *The Economist*, November 11, 2010.

[32] Data for 2010 from "Financial and Economic Data Relating to NATO Defence, Defence expenditures of NATO countries (1990–2010)," Table 3, Defence

Moreover, throughout Europe, most countries have been grappling with budget deficits, aging populations, and lagging economies, and this has resulted in reduced defense spending and troop levels.

Even these numbers do not convey the limits to Europe's capacity for burden sharing. Although the continent still has more men and women under arms than does the United States, the effective military capability is far less. The European members of NATO collectively maintain larger numbers of troops than the United States (2 million versus 1.4 million) and spend more on military personnel, but their capacity to equip, deploy, and sustain soldiers on operations is much lower than that of America. In addition, the weapons and communications systems for many of these troops are less advanced than those deployed by the United States, so that close coordination in operations becomes more difficult.

Europeans, led by Britain and France, played a crucial role in leading the Libyan intervention from March to October 2011. They also have led important peacekeeping missions in sub-Saharan Africa and the Balkans. In Afghanistan, nearly one-third of coalition forces were provided by NATO members other than the United States. Even so, with the exception of the British, the Canadians, the Danes, and a few others, many of the European contingents operated under restricted rules of engagement. These forces were useful for peacekeeping, stability, and training, and their presence helped strengthen the legitimacy of the overall Afghanistan operation as it was perceived internationally and by the American public. On the other hand, in Libya, the Europeans were hard-pressed to sustain their commitment, even though it involved no regular ground troops, and they had to call on the United States for ammunition, helicopters, transport and surveillance aircraft, air-to-air refueling, drones, and target identification.

Ironically, the political dynamic in transatlantic relations has shifted noticeably over the course of the past decade. Previously, the enlargement and deepening of the European Union, followed by growing friction over the perceived uses of American power and then the war in Iraq, led some European leaders and more than a few public

expenditures as a percentage of gross domestic product, NATO Public Diplomacy Division, Brussels, Belgium, Press Release (2011) 027, Issued March 10, 2011, http://www.nato.int/cps/en/natolive/news_71296.htm?mode=pressrelease, accessed November 28, 2011.

intellectuals, pundits, and academics to announce that Europe would soon be counterbalancing against the United States. Plans for enhancing Europe's collective military capability, including the Common Security and Defense Policy, formation of EU battle groups capable of foreign intervention, and the development of European weapons systems, including the A-400 transport aircraft and the Galileo GPS system, were meant to demonstrate Europe's growing ability to operate without being so completely reliant on the United States.

Embodying this narrative, one widely quoted American academic predicted an outright rupture between Europe and America, writing that "The central question . . . is thus not how to repair the transatlantic relationship, but whether the end of the alliance will take the form of an amicable separation or a nasty divorce."[33] In addition, he argued that within a decade, Europe would possess both the capability and the political coherence to become an alternative pole of world power. However, this vision was never really shared among European leaders. Although support for this notion of Europe as superpower was briefly evident in France, Germany, and some of the continental countries, especially in 2003–2004, at the height of disagreement over Iraq, elsewhere, especially in Britain, Eastern Europe, the Netherlands, and Scandinavia, there was reluctance to assert distance from America. In any case, the impetus for counterbalancing soon evaporated. In 2005, rejection of the proposed European Constitutional Treaty by the voters of the Netherlands and France delivered a shock. The subsequent Lisbon Treaty proved a weaker basis for policy and institutional cooperation in an unwieldy EU of twenty-seven countries. Beginning in 2008, successive crises in finance, banking, and the Eurozone left Europe weakened and in disarray. Coupled with Europe's structural problems, aging populations, and soaring budget deficits, the result was a far more restrained sense of Europe's possibilities.[34]

---

[33] Charles Kupchan, *The End of the American Era* (New York: Vintage, 2003), p. 151.
[34] For example, Timothy Garton Ash, "European Union: Everywhere You Look, a Crisis," *Los Angeles Times*, June 16, 2011. Also, for a reversal by one of those who had been most expansive about Europe just a few years earlier, see Charles Kupchan, "*The Potential Twilight of the European Union*" (Washington, DC: Council on Foreign Relations Working Paper), September 2010, http://www.cfr. org/content/publications/attachments/IIGG_Eurozone_WorkingPaper_Kupchan.pdf, accessed July 11, 2011.

The fact that American military primacy relative to Europe has increased is not a trend to applaud. As evidence of this shift, U.S. defense spending now represents 75 percent of NATO's total, compared with 50 percent during the Cold War. The United States needs allies for burden sharing, yet the less capable they are, the greater the weight of responsibilities the United States has to bear and hence the risk of overextension.

By contrast, the situation among America's Asian allies differs considerably from that in Europe. Whereas European governments and populations mostly perceive a decreased sense of threat and in the face of budget pressures are choosing to reduce spending on forces and weapons, China's muscle flexing and rapid military expansion is having the opposite effect in Asia. There, Australia, Indonesia, India, Japan, Singapore, South Korea, and Vietnam have reacted by ramping up their own military modernization programs and purchases of advanced weapons systems. They are embarked on upgrading hardware, technology, aircraft, and naval forces, and they are reaching out more overtly to the United States for deterrence and reassurance vis-à-vis China. While China's rapidly expanding military capability poses a regional threat, the combined weight of its neighbors plus American forces provides a counterbalance.

Limits of Global Governance

As an accompaniment or outright alternative to American leadership, almost every deliberation about foreign policy gives rise to calls for renewed or enhanced reliance on international institutions and multilateralism as the preferred means for addressing common problems.[35] Among observers who foresee American decline, some clearly welcome this. These happy-declinists are not bothered by the prospect, both because they undervalue American predominance and because they overestimate the possibilities for global cooperation.[36] From this

---

[35] This section expands on an analysis in Robert J. Lieber, "Persistent Primacy and the Future of the American Era," *International Politics* (London), Vol. 46, No. 2/3 (March 2009): 125–127.

[36] As an example of panglossian declinism, see Charles Kenny, "Three Cheers for Decline," *Foreignpolicy.com*, August 9, 2011, http://www.foreignpolicy.com/articles/2011/08/09/three_cheers_for_decline, accessed August 23, 2011.

perspective, the emergence and expansion of international norms and regimes is seen as evidence of growing global governance, thus lessening the need and appropriateness of a primarily national approach. The UN and its specialized agencies are pointed to, and global, functional, or regional bodies such as the International Atomic Energy Commission (IAEA), World Trade Organization (WTO), and the European Union (EU) are praised for their roles above and beyond the nation-state. And for some, authorization by the United Nations Security Council has come to be regarded as the litmus test for any foreign intervention.

Of course, international law operates in multiple realms, and traditional national sovereignty has eroded under pressure from the forces of modernity and globalization. This is especially true for smaller and medium-sized countries and for rules and practices involving trade, finance, investment, intellectual property, civil aviation, shipping, and sports. To some extent this internationalization also applies to peacekeeping (although not to peacemaking) and to international tribunals used to punish a selected number of gross human rights violators from conflicts in places such as Bosnia, Rwanda, and Liberia.

Shared understandings and rules of the road are important, but by no means do all societies accept the norms of liberal democracy, transparency, and the rule of law. Moreover, even shared norms and beliefs can be flawed. Why, for example, is a decision to act against threats to the peace more legitimate when it is validated by the representatives of authoritarian regimes in Moscow and Beijing than when merely agreed to by the elected leaders of liberal democracies? In crisis situations, the invocation of global governance, international norms, or treaty obligations is as much or more likely to be a pretext for inaction than a spur to compliance. And the more urgent, dangerous, or deadly the peril, the less likely there is to be effective agreement by the international community.

Problems in collective action to cope with international crises, threats to the peace, failed states, and mass murder have repeatedly been evident in recent decades. Consider a number of cases in point:

- The Rwanda genocide of 1994, where the UN Security Council permanent members, led by the United States, consciously averted their gaze and deliberately reduced the small UN troop presence.

- Bosnia, from 1992 to 1995, where UN resolutions and peacekeepers proved unable to halt the carnage or to rein in Serbia, and where UN peacekeepers stood by impotently during the July 1995 Srebrenica massacre of some 7,000 Bosnian Muslim men and boys.
- Iraq under Saddam Hussein, which from 1991 to 2002 failed to comply with its obligations in sixteen successive UN Security Council resolutions passed under Chapter VII of the UN Charter and which from 1996 to 2002 used bribery and corruption to undermine the UN oil-for-food program and divert revenues for Saddam's use.
- North Korea, which has systematically flouted both IAEA and UN resolutions as well as its obligations under the Nuclear Nonproliferation Treaty (NPT).
- Iran, whose concealed nuclear program violated not only NPT and IAEA requirements for some two decades, but also at least four UN Security Council resolutions, and whose Revolutionary Guard Corps has intervened covertly in Lebanon and Iraq, and carried out terrorist bombings as far afield as Argentina.
- Sudan, whose depredations in the Darfur region caused as many as 400,000 deaths and the flight of some 2 million refugees, and which managed (with help from the Chinese) to minimize effective international intervention by the UN Security Council.
- Russia, which has used both overt and covert means to intimidate or coerce independent states of the former Soviet Union by arming separatist groups, refusing to withdraw its troops and bases, and manipulating energy supplies, and which launched a disproportionate attack against Georgia after that small republic reacted rashly to a series of provocations orchestrated by Moscow in the separatist enclave of South Ossetia.
- Syria and Hezbollah, which have repeatedly defied UN Security Council resolutions concerning Lebanese sovereignty and the disarming of militias. In addition, the Syrian regime of Bashar al-Assad has repeatedly used murderous violence against peaceful protesters while defying international criticism and limited sanctions.

Not all of these cases are threats to America's national security, interests, or allies, but they illustrate the limitations of the UN and mechanisms of global governance. At times it has been possible to work with allies outside the UN framework in responding effectively to crises. An instructive case was the 1999 agreement of NATO member states to intervene in Kosovo in order to halt ethnic cleansing and mass murder. This occurred after it had become clear that Russia would veto any UN Security Council authorization to act against Serbia. Many, although not all, international law experts saw the intervention as lacking international legitimation, but the American-led air war against Serbian forces in Kosovo and targets within Serbia itself ultimately brought ethnic cleansing to a halt. The NATO intervention, however, exhibited military and tactical limitations. The great majority of the air sorties were conducted by the Americans, with some participation by the British and other alliance air forces, but most of the NATO contingents lacked the advanced military technology and force deployments to be able to cooperate effectively with the U.S. Air Force.

Even when consensus can be reached by regional organizations and the UN, the problems of implementation remain daunting. A consequence of this phenomenon can be found in Libya. There, condemnation of the Qaddafi regime and its killing of civilians during the mass protests and uprising that began in March 2011 led to resolutions in the Arab League and the Organization of the Islamic Conference condemning those actions and calling for a no-fly zone to protect civilians. The UN Security Council followed suit, with Resolution 1973, demanding an immediate ceasefire in Libya, an end to attacks against civilians (which it said might constitute "crimes against humanity"), a ban on all flights in the country's airspace, and tightened sanctions on the Qaddafi regime and its supporters. The Council resolution called on the Arab League's member states to cooperate in implementing the no-fly zone and, most importantly, it authorized member states to take "all necessary measures" to protect civilians – diplomatic language for the use of force.[37]

Despite the seeming consensus and international authority set out in the UN's Libya resolution, events yet again reflected the difficulties of organizing and conducting collective action. The resolution had been

---

[37] "Security Council Approves 'No-Fly Zone' over Libya, Authorizing 'All Necessary Measures' to Protect Civilians, by Vote of 10 in Favour with 5 Abstentions," http://www.un.org/News/Press/docs/2011/sc10200.doc.htm, accessed April 23, 2011.

adopted by a vote of ten in favor and none against. However, five countries abstained, including Germany, the largest and most economically powerful member of the EU, and four of the BRICS (Brazil, Russia, India, China; South Africa voted in favor). The abstention of all but one of the BRICS testifies yet again to the reticence of these countries toward collective action, common values, and liberal order, as well as their limited capacity to project power.[38] In short, international consensus only goes so far.

In the days that followed, France and Britain, who had taken the lead in summoning international action, conducted air strikes against Qaddafi's forces. The effort was bolstered temporarily by a wave of American missile and air attacks against the Libyan dictator's air force and air defenses, in what the Obama administration labeled "Operation Odyssey Dawn." Very soon, however, in the absence of American leadership and full-fledged engagement, the limits of collective action became apparent. Despite calling for Qaddafi's ouster, President Obama insisted that his only commitment was to protect civilians, that U.S. forces would pull back to a supporting role, there would be no "boots on the ground," and command of the operation would be turned over to NATO. Problems with this formula soon became obvious. Some NATO countries (Germany and Turkey) were very reluctant about the combat mission and the expansive definition of protecting civilians. And while a number of NATO countries did join the air operations, their involvement was limited by political restrictions or by vastly lesser capabilities than those of the Americans. As then-Secretary of Defense Robert Gates acidly observed, all twenty-eight NATO members had voted for the intervention, yet fewer than half contributed forces and less than a third conducted air strikes. In his words, "The mightiest military alliance in history is only 11 weeks into an operation against a poorly armed regime in a sparsely populated country – yet many allies are beginning to run short of munitions, requiring the U.S., once more, to make up the difference."[39]

---

[38] Jorge Castaneda makes this point effectively in "The Trouble with the BRICS," *Foreign Policy*, March 14, 2011. *Foreignpolicy.com*, http://www.foreignpolicy.com/articles/2011/03/14/the_trouble_with_the_brics, accessed August 23, 2011.

[39] Secretary of Defense Robert M. Gates, "The Security and Defense Agenda (Future of NATO)," speech delivered in Brussels, Belgium, June 10, 2011, http://www.defense.gov/speeches/speech.aspx?speechid=1581, accessed July 11, 2011.

A few non-NATO countries did make modest contributions in Libya. Qatar and the United Arab Emirates provided a limited number of aircraft to monitor the no-fly zone, and Qatar deployed liaisons to operate on the ground with some rebel units. In addition, Turkey organized a sea evacuation of refugees and the wounded from the besieged city of Misrata. The eventual breakthrough by rebel forces, their capture of Qaddafi's stronghold in Tripoli, and victory over regime forces came only after the United States and NATO sharply increased their air attacks on Qaddafi's forces.

Compared with the NATO operation in Kosovo a dozen years earlier, alliance limitations were increasingly evident. Moreover, with a reduced U.S. role, declining capabilities on the part of European NATO members, and fewer alliance countries taking an active part, the tempo of operations was much slower than in Kosovo. In Libya, NATO forces deployed many fewer aircraft and, on a daily basis, they averaged less than one-fourth the number of air sorties undertaken during the Kosovo operation. For the Obama administration, the lower profile offered both advantages and disadvantages. On the one hand, working with allies and with Britain and France in the lead, it eventually brought the desired outcome – the fall of Qaddafi's detestable regime. At a time of extensive military commitments elsewhere and with the prospect of limited public support for intervention, American ground troops did not have to be committed to the operation, nor were there U.S. military casualties. In addition, the cost of the operation amounted to less than $1 billion. Not a small sum, but minimal in contrast with America's recent wars.

Whether this exercise in "leading from behind" could serve as a template for future American strategy was much less certain. Although the rebels prevailed, allied operations against Qaddafi's weak, underequipped military, mostly located in a narrow strip of the Mediterranean coastline easily accessible to European and U.S. air and naval forces, took nearly six months, whereas stronger and more decisive initial attacks might have brought Qaddafi's defeat much more quickly and at less human cost. European capabilities alone were insufficient, and American weapons, technology, air assets, and intelligence proved to be indispensable. Overall, the United States still provided at least one-fourth of the total air sorties. Against a more formidable threat, this limited role would almost certainly have been inadequate. In addition, the future stability of Libya remained uncertain, as did control of its chemical munitions and the remaining radioactive materials from its abandoned nuclear program. Finally, domestic support for Libya policy was problematic. The president did not seek congressional approval, claiming it was unnecessary because U.S. forces were not engaged in hostilities, and public opinion turned heavily against the Libya operation as weeks and then months passed.

Unipolarity and Apolarity

In view of the NATO allies' diminished resources for power projection, their capacity for burden sharing remains limited. To be sure, some observers continue to express more expansive views about Europe's capacity. Thus Andrew Moravcsik of Princeton labels Europe the "Second Superpower" (after the United States) and insists that "Europe has established itself unambiguously as the world's 'second' military power, with combat troops active across the globe."[40] Notwithstanding such assessments, most Europeans deployed abroad are present as observers or peacekeepers rather than in a combat role, and national military capabilities have been shrinking. European leaders have chosen to squeeze their own defense budgets and that constraint is worsening as a consequence of demography, rising costs of aging populations, complacency about external security threats, and the politics of coalition governments for whom defense spending is a low priority.

In the meantime, the BRICS and other rising regional powers have shown little inclination to take responsibility for meeting common world problems, whether in response to humanitarian intervention, assisting failed states, nuclear proliferation, free trade, the international monetary system, global climate change, or combating HIV/AIDS. Thus the alternative to American involvement on these and other issues is unlikely to be the assumption of responsibility by other powers or by regional bodies and the UN. The consequence should the United States pull back markedly from its accustomed international role is much more likely to be a disorderly and conflict-prone world rather than one with growing levels of cooperation and global governance.

[40] Andrew Moravcsik, "Europe, the Second Superpower," *Current History* (March 2010): 91–98, at 92.

For the United States, the wars in Iraq and Afghanistan have been costly in human and material terms. While gradual drawdowns of U.S. forces take place, future stability in Iraq cannot be taken for granted, and Afghanistan is an open question at best. Meanwhile, there is no shortage of other lands where American commitment is either ongoing or likely to be called on in some way. Among these, containing a nuclear Iran is likely to require assurances to Teheran's neighbors. Then there are the burdens of combating a weakened but still dangerous al-Qaeda and radical jihadist groups in Yemen. Added to these is a fraught relationship with a nuclear Pakistan, where future risks could dwarf those elsewhere in the region. In East Asia, maintaining credible deterrence and reassurance for China's neighbors requires continued deployment of substantial American forces. And on the home front there remains a need to update and modernize weaponry and delivery systems worn by the rigors of two long and distant wars.

Affordability presents a paradox. Current defense spending appears high in absolute terms, though declining as a percentage of GDP and is projected to drop with the withdrawals from Iraq and Afghanistan. As noted in this chapter's section on military costs and capabilities, by historical standards these outlays seem relatively manageable when compared with percentages during the past seven decades. The ultimate question is not whether the United States can afford substantial levels of expenditure, but whether competing domestic priorities may impose tenacious constraints. From this perspective, the share of defense spending as a portion of the federal budget (where debt service and entitlements take up a rapidly increasing share) may be as important as the percentage of GDP itself.

Commitments and Political Sustainability

Overall, the burdens of America's world role are substantial but do not in and of themselves represent overstretch. The underlying question is more likely to be whether the American public and its political elites will continue to support these commitments or instead conclude that resource constraints and other priorities require a fundamental reorientation. Here, public attitudes toward the use of force provide a key indicator of political sustainability. As noted in Chapters 2 and 3, opinion polls have consistently shown a willingness among the public to contemplate the use of force. A broader indication can be found in response to a *Transatlantic Trends* survey question on whether the United States should exert strong leadership in world affairs. Among the general public, 82 percent approved.[41]

A more ambiguous indicator of American attitudes can be found in the initial reactions to the U.S. air and missile strikes in Libya. A March 2011 Gallup poll found 47 percent of respondents approving while 37 percent disapproved, a far lower level of support than for prior American military actions. In contrast, intervention in Libya a quarter-century earlier, at the time of the Reagan administration's April 1986 bombing of Qaddafi's compound in Tripoli, had earned a 71-to-21 margin of support. The post-9/11 intervention in Afghanistan received overwhelming 90-to-5 approval, and even the hotly disputed March 2003 Operation Iraqi Freedom had initial support from 76 percent of the public, with only 20 percent disapproving.[42]

Though the decision to use force in Libya had lower approval ratings than previous military actions, poll respondents exhibited little sign of serious political polarization. Among the public at large, Democrats approved the action 51 percent versus 34 percent, and Republicans by a margin of 57 percent to 31 percent. Only independents disapproved, 38 percent in favor, 44 percent against. However, opinion soon shifted against the intervention, and by mid-August, shortly before the rebels finally took Qaddafi's headquarters in Tripoli, only 20 percent of likely voters still supported the military action.[43]

The results of these and other surveys provide additional evidence that the public is skeptical about military intervention where national security interests do not seem to be at stake, although Americans will support action where there is a greater sense of threat and necessity. Thus both public opinion and resource constraints create incentives

[41] *Transatlantic Trends*, "Survey: Leaders More Optimistic on Transatlantic Relations Than General Public," March 15, 2011, http://trends.gmfus.org/?page_id=2971, accessed April 29, 2011.

[42] Jeffrey M. Jones, "Americans Approve of Military Action Against Libya, 47% to 37%" *Gallup.com*, March 22, 2011, http://www.gallup.com/poll/146738/Americans-Approve-Military-Action-Against-Libya.aspx, accessed April 25, 2011.

[43] "20% Now Support U.S. Military Action in Libya," *Rasmmussenreports.com*, August 17, 2011, http://www.rasmussenreports.com/public_content/politics/general_politics/august_2011/20_now_support_u_s_military_action_in_libya, accessed August 23, 2011.

for careful judgment and a keen sense of priorities in foreign policy commitments and the use of force. Here, too, the ability of America to sustain its international role and to avoid the decline of its domestic base is less a question of material limits, including the existing burdens it carries in foreign affairs, than it is of judgment, will, and leadership.

6

Power and Willpower in the American Future

"Americans can always be counted on to do the right thing . . . after they have exhausted all other possibilities."

– Winston Churchill

America now faces formidable problems at home and abroad. This predicament is not entirely new. In previous eras the country surmounted severe crises, and it is important not to underestimate resilience and adaptability. Current concerns need to be seen against a history of pessimistic assessments, as, for example, during the Depression of the 1930s, the post-Vietnam era of the late 1970s, and again in the late 1980s when beliefs about Japan as "number one" and of the emergent EU as a world power were widely held. This suggests a common tendency to undervalue America's fundamental strengths and its ability to overcome adversity. Yet even those most optimistic about the American future must ask themselves whether this time it is different.[1]

This concluding chapter begins with that question and then weighs the country's persistent strengths and the critical importance of ideas, beliefs, and policies. The material aspects of national power matter

---

[1] In a recent book asking this question, two well-respected economists examine a wide range of financial crises across sixty-six countries and eight centuries and find important commonalities in these cases of financial disaster. See Carmen M. Reinhart and Kenneth S. Rogoff, *This Time Is Different: Eight Centuries of Financial Folly* (Princeton, NJ: Princeton University Press, 2009).

greatly, but they shape outcomes only in very broad terms. Ultimately, it is the choices made about policy and strategy that are crucial. America's future is a matter of will and willpower, in the sense that successful responses to our problems depend on purposeful and concerted action to address our most serious problems. Willpower in particular involves leadership and the willingness to make well-informed and wise decisions. Provided the necessary choices are made, there are compelling reasons to anticipate that the robustness of American society, coupled with its unique capacities for adaptation and adjustment, will once again prove decisive.

Is This Time Different?

The record of the past is impressive, suggesting deep inherent strengths in American society, but this cumulative history provides no certainty. It is thus necessary to ask whether current realities are different and major challenges at home and abroad may not be so effectively surmounted.

At the international level, the diffusion of power is real. We now live in a much more globalized world, in which the countries of the Atlantic world are no longer so dominant, while emerging powers, especially in Asia, are rapidly gaining in importance. Formidable economic competition and the migration of advanced technologies and manufacturing abroad, especially to China, is the most prominent feature of this trend, and Beijing's enormous trade surpluses and amassing of some $3 trillion worth of reserves constitutes a major source of financial power and influence. In recent years, an increasingly self-confident, economically dynamic, and irredentist China has been rapidly expanding its modern military capacity and now poses a growing regional and potentially global threat. In the face of this challenge, the United States might be far less capable of playing the stabilizing role it has exercised since World War II.

In addition, failed states, insurgencies, asymmetrical wars, nuclear proliferation, terrorism, and Islamist radicalism pose threats that may be less susceptible to traditional uses of American power and influence. International institutions are more pluralized in membership and less responsive to Washington's leadership than was the case in past decades. Additionally, America's traditional European allies, with their aging populations, economic difficulties, and reduced military forces, are now significantly weaker in their ability and willingness to project power alongside the United States.

On the domestic front, there may also be problems that differ in nature and scope from past experience. The most important of these are the fiscal imbalances that threaten America's economic future as well as its ability to project power abroad. Although the United States has recovered from previous economic and financial crises, the current size of the fiscal deficit and the needs of an aging population and of entitlement programs for health care and retirement constrain the options available to policy makers. Recovery from the collapse of the housing bubble continues to be protracted, and traditional policy tools for reducing unemployment and stimulating economic growth are seemingly less effective than past experience would suggest. Questions have also been raised about whether, in view of the cumbersome nature of the federal government and its bureaucracy, it is even capable of managing these tasks.

Domestic political polarization may also make it more difficult to reach agreement on the necessary policy measures to cope with problems of debt, deficit, and entitlements. Not only is Congress more polarized than at any time since 1879, but deep partisan divisions are evident among voters who self-identify with the major parties. Presidential approval ratings during the Clinton, Bush, and Obama presidencies have shown dramatic differences based on party affiliation. For example, Gallup and other surveys have shown gaps of as much as 65 percent to 70 percent between Democrats and Republicans on favorability ratings of the Obama presidency.[2]

Serious economic and political problems also exist at state levels. Entitlement programs and unmanageable retirement costs for government employees have left some states in dire financial condition.

---

[2] For example, at the beginning of May 2011, President Obama's job approval among Democrats stood at 80%, versus 10% among Republicans – a 70% difference. In the aftermath of the successful operation to kill Bin Laden, the President's popularity improved modestly, with 83% support from Democrats and 21% from Republicans. Yet by June 1, the partisan gap had widened again (82% vs. 15%) – a difference of 67%. Jeffrey M. Jones, "Obama Approval Rally Largely Over," *Gallup.com*, June 15, 2011, http://www.gallup.com/poll/148046/Obama-Approval-Rally-Largely .aspx?version=print, accessed June 17, 2011.

California is a special case in point because for much of the past century it has been both an example and leader in social trends. But the Golden State faces enormous and as yet unresolved problems of budget deficits and unfunded pension liabilities. It labors under severe restrictions on its ability to raise taxes, reform state employee health and retirement programs, manage a welter of environmental, tax, and regulatory policies that discourage business investment, and cope with a massive influx of undocumented (that is, illegal) immigrants from Mexico and Central America.

These problems – and more – fuel the many prophecies of American decline. It would be a mistake, however, to assume that these provide a definitive picture of the American future. This is especially evident in comparisons of the United States with other once dominant powers. Historians and pundits are fond of comparing the United States in its current predicament with the declining fortunes of the British Empire. Although seemingly plausible, the analogy breaks down when we look at the evidence. A century ago, in the years prior to the outbreak of World War I, Britain had already been surpassed in GDP and steel production by Germany and the United States, in size of standing army by Germany, in population by Russia, Germany, and the United States, and even in the realm it had long dominated – sea power – the United States and Germany were beginning to challenge.[3] In short, even though it headed an empire that covered a quarter of the world's land area and population and was the world's leading imperial power, it was no longer dominant in its relative status. The fate of empires notwithstanding, the United States does not rule over foreign lands and is not an empire, although the label is often invoked by critics of American policies and purpose.

America's Edge

America's advantages include both material and nonmaterial elements. Many of these have been cited in the previous chapters, but it is worthwhile to reference them here because they offset much of the declinist case. For example, economic problems figure prominently

---

[3] Aaron L. Friedberg, *The Weary Titan: Britain and the Experience of Relative Decline 1895–1905* (Princeton, NJ: Princeton University Press, rev. ed., 2010), pp. 26 and 153.

in assessments of the American future. Nevertheless, despite difficulties of recovering from the worst financial and housing crises since the 1930s, according to IMF data, the United States still accounts for some 21 percent of world GDP, only slightly lower than the 26 percent figure it represented in 1980.[4] Even if less favorable purchasing power parity (PPP) data are used, the American share amounts to 18.7 percent, as contrasted with 24.6 percent in 1980. These figures illustrate a fundamental point. They reflect an identifiable but modest erosion in the relative standing of the United States compared to that of other countries; however, at the same time, they attest to America's status as still by a substantial margin the world's largest economy.

In assessing material strength, total GDP figures are considerably less important than per capita GDP. Not only does the United States remain far ahead of other major countries, but as noted in Chapter 2, America's per capita GDP is more than five times greater than that of China and will remain well ahead for a very long time.[5] Moreover, the United States remains the world's largest consumer market, has the deepest capital markets, benefits from the dollar's role as the world's predominant reserve currency, and despite a large trade deficit is the world's third-largest exporter of goods and services as well as the largest importer.

Additional material factors underpin the American advantage. The country covers a vast land area and is far less densely populated than its major competitors. It possesses enormous natural resources, including large reserves of minerals as well as coal and natural gas. It is the world's third-largest producer of oil after Saudi Arabia and Russia, and thanks to advances in technology for extracting shale gas and tight oil, its production of both is increasing. It is also one of the world's leading agricultural producers. It enjoys a higher fertility rate among women than any other major country except India. With its

---

[4] The estimated figure for 2012 was 21.01%. Data from International Monetary Fund, *World Economic Outlook Database*, September 2011, http://www.imf.org/external/pubs/ft/weo/2011/02/weodata/index.aspx, accessed October 29, 2011.

[5] China's per capita GDP is only $9,204 per person whereas that of the U.S. is $49,055. Data for 2012 from International Monetary Fund, *World Economic Outlook Database*, September 2010, http://www.imf.org/external/pubs/ft/weo/2011/02/weodata/index.aspx, accessed November 29, 2011. See also Michael Beckley, "China's Century?" *International Security*, Vol. 36, No. 3 (Winter 2011/12), forthcoming.

population, birth rates, and immigration, the United States benefits from a growing population and workforce. Based on aggregate data from Gallup surveys conducted in recent years and covering 148 countries, the United States remains by far the most popular destination for immigrants.[6]

While other countries seek to develop their own high-tech sectors, Silicon Valley remains unique, and clusters of technological innovation and development flourish around many of the country's major research universities. In addition, the United States remains well positioned to advance in cutting-edge areas of technology including medicine, biotechnology, gene therapy, nanotechnology, and clean energy.

Nonmaterial factors are central to America's position. The society's resilience and adaptability are unusual for a large country and these facilitate its response to new challenges. Economic competitiveness and entrepreneurship continue to be key assets. Major research universities are still unmatched by other countries, and the United States enrolls a higher proportion of the world's international students than any other country. Even with the expansion of universities in Europe, Asia, and elsewhere, the American lead in post-baccalaureate education remains extraordinary. Some two-thirds of graduate students who study abroad do so in the United States.[7] The English language provides yet another built-in advantage, which contributes to an extensive cultural influence. This includes high, medium, and low culture, ranging from the construction of major museums based on American models, as in the case of the Guggenheim in Bilbao and another being constructed in Abu Dhabi, to the extensive spread of Hollywood films abroad, and to the diffusion of video games and of less edifying forms of music (for example, "gangsta rap").

---

[6] Among those who indicated they would like to move permanently if they had the chance, 24% choose the United States, trailed by Canada and the United Kingdom at 7% each, France with 6%, and Spain, Saudi Arabia, Germany, and Australia at 4%. Based on data from surveys of 2007 and 2010 in "Worldwide Approval of U.S. Leadership Tops Major Powers," March 24, 2011, http://www.gallup.com/poll/146771/Worldwide-Approval-Leadership-Tops-Major-Powers.aspx?utm_source=alert&utm_medium=email&utm_campaign=syndication&utm_content=morelink&utm_term=Presidential%20Job%20Approval%20-%20The%20Presidency, accessed June 8, 2011. Also see Jeremy Page, "Many Rich Chinese Consider Leaving," *Wall Street Journal*, November 2, 2011.

[7] Data cited in "The Global Campus," *The Economist*, January 22, 2011.

Democracy constitutes a fundamental strength. This includes the rule of law, liberty, and popular sovereignty. There is no doubt that the democratic process is often messy and raucous, but it makes the political system responsive to a huge and heterogeneous public. It is well to keep in mind that America's main peer competitor, China, lacks these vital features. As a consequence, China is sooner or later likely to experience major crises. There the gap between the rulers and the ruled could become increasingly untenable for a wealthier, more educated population with access to information and social media and increasingly aware of its own lack of political and civil liberties and the arbitrariness and absence of accountability of those who control political power. Indeed, according to some accounts, China may be experiencing as many as 180,000 political, civil, or labor disturbances per year.[8] Another telltale sign comes in a survey of China's "high net worth individuals," defined as those with more than 10 million yuan (slightly more than $1.5 million) in investable assets, almost 60 percent of whom responded either that they are considering emigration via investment programs in foreign countries or else are completing the process.[9]

Ideas, Beliefs, and Policies

Matters of belief are often subsumed within debates about policy, without receiving the explicit attention they deserve. But ideas are crucial because they shape both our understanding of America itself and of the choices open to it. On the domestic side, we need to consider core assumptions both about the economy and the wider society, as well as America's basic strengths and weaknesses. In foreign policy, a related set of considerations applies, especially beliefs about America's capacity to act, the character of the role that it has and should play, and

---

[8] Andrew Jacobs, "Village Revolts Over Irregularities of Chinese Life," *New York Times*, December 14, 2011. Also see "My Children Have Been Poisoned," Human Rights Watch, June 15, 2011, http://www.hrw.org/en/reports/2011/06/15/my-children-have-been-poisoned, accessed June 20, 2011.

[9] The survey conducted by China Merchants Bank and Bain & Co. is cited in Gordon C. Chang, "Chinese Entrepreneurs Are Leaving China," *Blogs.Forbes.com*, June 5, 2011, http://blogs.forbes.com/gordonchang/2011/06/05/chinese-entrepreneurs-are-leaving-china, accessed June 8, 2011.

the tension between national priorities and international institutions. Moreover, assuming the United States does have the capacity to act, should it do so and in what form?

How to proceed in coping with domestic problems depends on policy preferences as well as assumptions about the underlying robustness of the economy and society. For example, is government action the solution or the problem? What is the optimal mix of governmental policy and private initiative? Are we optimistic or pessimistic about economic recovery, growth, and innovation? To what extent can government policies create suitable incentives and disincentives to encourage desired results?

Notions about the character of American society are fundamental too. As noted in Chapter 1, interpretations that paint U.S. history and society in an unrelentingly negative light are often embodied in ideas of political correctness in many school and college curricula. Authors, public figures, and activists such as the late Howard Zinn, filmmaker Michael Moore, and former radical underground leaders William Ayres and Bernadine Dohrn come to mind, but there are many others who prioritize concepts of race, class, and gender to the detriment of broader concerns. For those who interpret American society in a pejorative way, American decline is taken as given, not only as a description of reality, but even as something to be desired.

Views about American exceptionalism come into play here as well. If one accepts that there is something unique about the society and its founding values, there is likely to be greater optimism about its resilience and the importance of its global role. On this subject, much has been made about Barack Obama's ambiguous response, "I believe in American exceptionalism, just as I suspect that the Brits believe in British exceptionalism and the Greeks believe in Greek exceptionalism."[10] It may seem excessive to dwell on this offhand remark, but the choice of words reflects diffidence about the role and uses of American power.

Beliefs about foreign policy need to be understood in both substantive and normative terms. Substantively, judgments about the

---

[10] President Obama's response to a reporter's question at the G-20 Summit, Strasbourg, France, April 4, 2009. Quoted in James Kirchick, "Squanderer in Chief," *Los Angeles Times*, April 28, 2009.

capacity of the United States to engage and lead abroad rest on estimates of its underlying strength and resources. For example, Michael
Mandelbaum's sober treatment in *The Frugal Superpower* (discussed
in Chapter 2) emphasizes the financial constraints that debt and deficit
entail and lead him to conclude that significant retrenchment in foreign policy is unavoidable. However, if Mandelbaum's assessment is
too pessimistic and the United States instead is able to achieve sufficient
economic growth and to manage its problems with deficits and entitlements, then there is reason for greater optimism about its capacity
for continued leadership abroad.

Beyond calculations of guns versus butter, underlying normative
judgments about America's world role mirror those about domestic
society. Criticisms of American foreign policy have come in cycles,
notably in reaction to the Vietnam War and, a generation later, the
war in Iraq. A limited amount of outright isolationist sentiment can
be found on the far right of the political spectrum, for example in
the writings of Patrick Buchanan and in the pages of *The American Conservative* magazine, or in the libertarian positions of those
such as Representative Ron Paul. For others, especially on the left,
America's role abroad is viewed with deep suspicion. Public intellectuals such as Noam Chomsky have only sweeping denunciation to
offer, to the extent that actions against even the most violent and
deadly foreign adversaries, as in the killing of Osama bin Laden, elicit
condemnation. For others, less ideologically driven, skepticism about
what can be achieved and the costs of foreign involvement are more
central.

More sophisticated arguments concern international institutions
and ideas about global governance. Here, a reluctance to lead is condi-
tioned by beliefs that bodies such as the UN, the International Atomic
Energy Agency, or the International Criminal Court can or should
have the authority and capacity to act, and thus there is reluctance to
see the United States step forward without the action first having been
legitimized by one or more of these bodies.

National resources and political will are vital, yet presidential leadership is especially important. Examples from past presidencies in times
of crisis abound: George Washington, Abraham Lincoln, Franklin
Roosevelt during the Great Depression and World War II, as well as
Harry Truman in his administration's early years and Ronald Reagan

during the last decade of the Cold War. In this regard, the Truman presidency (1945–1953) provides an especially striking example of leadership in a period when unexpected events and uncertainties required imagination, composure, and a willingness to act decisively whatever the political costs. Truman is well known for major decisions, among them the use of the atomic bomb against Hiroshima and Nagasaki in order to end World War II in the Pacific, aid to Greece and Turkey during the earliest years of the Cold War (the Truman Doctrine), the dispatch of troops to Korea after the North Korean invasion in June 1950, and in April 1951 the firing of General Douglas MacArthur, commander of allied forces in Korea, for insubordination. However, as Adam Garfinkle has written, Truman's character and beliefs were especially noteworthy in three other decisions he made in 1948, each of which was politically controversial and a matter of dispute among advisors and policy elites. One was his May 1948 diplomatic recognition of Israel moments after it had declared its independence. Also in June of that year, he backed the advice of the commander of U.S. forces in Germany to defy the Soviet blockade of West Berlin. And in July of that years, he issued an Executive Order requiring the integration of America's armed forces. Each of these decisions was of major consequence, none was foreordained by material circumstances, and each required the exercise of both judgment and leadership.[11]

What Is to Be Done at Home

The list of potentially desirable measures to reduce or counteract the risks of decline is lengthy and daunting. Some of these are hardy perennials and have been invoked by reformers for decades, even generations. The ideas range from educational reform to overhauling job training, reductions in special-interest influence in Washington, and curbing waste, fraud, and abuse in government. Yet the problems to which these proposals are addressed have been stubborn features of American life in good times and bad, and are unlikely to be solved anytime soon. Other major steps are central to the American future and it is in these areas that change is essential. The most important

---

[11] Adam Garfinkle, "Here's to You, Harry," *The American Interest* (July/August 2008): 129–131.

areas include debt, the deficit, and entitlements, with closely related health care and tax reforms, as well as changes in immigration policy and measures to lessen dependence on imported oil.

Among these, debt, the deficit, and entitlements stand out. Solutions are both indispensable and feasible, and failure to achieve them would accelerate the kind of decline at home and abroad that pessimists and declinists foresee for the United States. The gap between what the federal government spends – approximately 25 percent of GDP – and what it takes in – less than 18 percent of GDP – is unsustainable. Moreover, an aging population and the retirement of the Baby Boom generation are likely to worsen these trends. In order to enact essential reforms, Congress and the president will have to reach agreement, and core Democratic and Republican constituencies will need to relax intensely held policy preferences. For Democrats, this means acquiescing on serious cuts and cost containment measures for government spending and entitlement programs including Medicare, Medicaid, and Social Security. For Republicans, this will require acceptance of measures to increase government revenues as part of tax reform. In addition, there are likely to be constraints on defense spending and veterans' benefits.

A central element for any agreement that really makes a critical difference is the issue of health care. It is both the most important and the most difficult of the entitlement issues, and it stands out as the most common target for cost control. Whereas defense has peaked at 5.1 percent of GDP and is on a downward path toward 3.5 percent as spending on Iraq and Afghanistan declines, health care's share of the national income has been climbing relentlessly. In 2011, it amounted to more than 17.3 percent of GDP, almost half of that in the public sector, and it is on an upward trajectory.[12]

The sources of these rising costs lie in a dysfunctional system that predisposes participants toward increased spending. Most individuals, both those covered by Medicare as well those covered by private health insurance plans, benefit from nearly unlimited fee-for-service arrangements. Medicare, the single largest program, pays for almost

---

[12] The 17.3% figure is an estimate from Table 1, National Health Expenditure and Selected Economic Indicators, 2004–2019, *National Health Expenditure Projections 2009–2019*, The Centers for Medicare & Medicaid Services, https://www.cms.gov/NationalHealthExpendData/downloads/proj2009.pdf, accessed June 11, 2011.

everything, and neither patients nor doctors have effective incentives to control costs.

The result is an unsustainable trend. As an example, a typical American consumer now in his mid-fifties can, in retirement, be expected to cost the Medicare program more than three times the amount of money he contributed during his working life. Medicare spending in 2010 amounted to $520 billion, and, together with Medicaid, the two health programs consumed 26.5 percent of the federal budget, a share substantially greater than the 20 percent share taken by defense. Moreover, defense spending is declining when inflation is taken into account, while by 2016 Obama administration projections show Medicare and Medicaid spending exceeding 30 percent of the budget.[13]

A hugely disproportionate share of medical costs for those on Medicare and Medicaid, as well as costs for those covered by private insurance programs, takes place in the last six months of life. Among older Americans, many if not most have had the experience of seeing family members or friends in their final days subjected to elaborate medical procedures and enormously expensive hospital stays, even when such measures were to no avail.

The threat of medical malpractice lawsuits also remains a significant source of medical expense. High liability insurance premiums, especially for certain specialties, contribute to costs, but more important are the unwarranted tests and procedures ordered by doctors in order to practice defensive medicine and protect themselves against the risk of future lawsuits.

Remedies are not simple, but they exist. One step is to introduce more competition into the system. Another is to reform both Medicare and private insurance programs so that patients are motivated to be more cost conscious in their health care spending. An obvious but politically fraught measure is to require that the individual medical consumer incur a more substantial "co-pay." Thus users of Medicare would have an incentive not to demand extensive tests and medication at the first sign of a health problem, and to shop for the cost-efficient sources of medical care. For example, if he knew that his share of

---

[13] See Robert J. Samuelson. "Why We Must End Medicare 'As We Know It,'" *The Washington Post*, June 5, 2011.

the cost for a procedure might amount to a few hundred dollars, a weekend tennis player with a sore knee would be more likely to hesitate in demanding an MRI on Monday morning instead of waiting a few days to see whether the problem resolved itself.

The retirement age for Medicare eligibility could be extended beyond the current age of sixty-five to postpone the date at which the system trust fund will otherwise become insolvent. Effective tort reform to discourage abuses in medical malpractice lawsuits would reduce costs, too. Another especially controversial change would be to apply more stringent criteria for terminally ill patients in their final days and weeks of life, and for whom palliative care would be preferable to elaborate and ultimately futile medical procedures.

These and other measures raise divisive ethical and political issues. At the national level and in many state jurisdictions, trial lawyers have effectively lobbied against tort reform. Rational use of end-of-life medical care elicits rhetorical denunciations of "death panels." Attempts to control Medicare and Medicaid costs by placing more responsibility on older and ailing patients lend themselves to caricature in "Mediscare" tactics. A prime example can be found in a political ad televised during a 2011 special election to fill a House seat in upstate New York. With a Republican cost-containment proposal as its target, it showed a wheelchair patient being pushed to the edge of a mountaintop and then pitched over the edge. Other proposals become fodder for bitter partisan disputes, social class antagonism, and heated debates about cutting social spending versus taxing the rich and about central planning versus individual responsibility.

In the short run, effective change seems elusive and difficult. Deep partisan differences over health care make compromise solutions hard to achieve. For its part, the controversial Patient Protection and Affordable Care Act (PPACA), labeled ObamaCare by its critics, adds tens of millions of people to health care rolls, and is unlikely to deliver the needed cost containment. Not only is it subject to serious legal challenges; opponents have suggested the program could require an additional $1 trillion in its first decade.[14] Ultimately, given the scale of

---

[14] Martin Feldstein, "The Economy Is Worse Than You Think," *The Wall Street Journal*, June 8, 2011. Feldstein served as chairman of the Council of Economic Advisers under President Ronald Reagan.

national health care expenditures, policy makers will have little choice but to respond. Paradoxically, the longer they delay and the more serious the problems of both medical care and cost, the more likely it is that effective action will ultimately be unavoidable. Although there can be no certainty, it would be consistent with the American past if a long-overdue response and an ensuing severe crisis finally provided sufficient urgency for action.

Beyond the broad areas of health care and entitlement reform, other challenges loom. For the economy as a whole, reducing debt and deficits is critical, but reduction of uncertainty and fostering a climate conducive to investment and economic growth is vital too. This is especially relevant for tax reform and rationalization of the corporate tax. The United States has the second-highest corporate taxes in the world (after Taiwan); however, due to the complexity of the tax structure and to loopholes in the law, some corporations pay little or no tax, while for others the tax structure creates incentives for investment abroad rather than at home.

Excessive bureaucracy and government regulation are closely connected. Some degree of regulation is desirable and necessary in a modern economy, but excesses in bureaucratic structures, tedious permitting processes, arbitrary applications of labor, employment, and environmental law, and overlapping federal, state, and local jurisdictions have become legendary. A prominent example was the Boeing Corporation's struggle with the National Labor Relations Board (NLRB) to establish a second production line in South Carolina for the manufacture of its new 787 Dreamliner plane, against the wishes of the union that has jurisdiction at Boeing's facility in Washington State.

Beyond these and other accounts of disputes over business and economic development, a small local case from California exemplifies how frustrating and dysfunctional the regulatory process can be. The story concerns an entrepreneurial young Iranian immigrant, Homa Dashtaki, who sought to market her father's traditional yogurt made in the style of the old county, and to which she gave the brand name, "The White Moustache." She had spent a year acquiring permits from Orange County and for three months had been successfully selling small batches at local farmers' markets. Then she received a call from the California Department of Food and Agriculture (CDFA) telling her to close down or risk prosecution. *The Economist* magazine describes what happened next:

The core assumption behind the CDFA's rules . . . is that all dairy products are made from raw milk, thus requiring elaborate processes that involve proper pasteurization. The White Moustache, however, was making yogurt from milk that was already pasteurized. . . . Ms. Dashtaki thus hoped for a waiver. Absolutely not, replied the CDFA. . . .

The regulator demanded instead that Ms. Dashtaki set up a "Grade A" dairy plant, just as a large factory processing raw milk would be required to do. She was told to install, among other things, a "pasteurizer with a recorder", a "culture tank", and a "filler", which apparently also required a "mechanical capper" to screw lids on jars. When Ms. Dashtaki pointed out to the CDFA inspector that all this would alter – meaning ruin – the taste of her father's artisanal yogurt, the inspector agreed. But that does not fall within the remit of the state of California's dairy regulations.

. . . Then a licensing officer told her that the code does not permit milk to be pasteurized a second time. So "in order to comply with the order to re-pasteurize my already pasteurized milk, I would need to get exemption from the head of the CDFA," she explains. The tale thus went from Kafka to Catch-22.

Ms. Dashtaki would have been happy to label her yogurt – "This product does not meet CDFA codes". . . . Not allowed. The argument that her target audience consists of sophisticated gourmets at farmers' markets fell flat, too.

. . . Ms. Dashtaki is pondering whether to move to another state, one whose rules allow for artisanal products. . . . Or she might just give up.[15]

Contrasts between the experiences of California and Texas suggest that economic growth and employment benefit when the legal and regulatory frameworks are practical and transparent. The two states are roughly comparable in population, diversity, and size. California is the largest state in the country, with 37 million people, while Texas is second, with nearly 25 million. Yet in the past decade, Texas has enjoyed a booming economy and has added more than 700,000 jobs, while California has lost 600,000. California, however, imposes some of the

---

[15] "Red Tape in California: Beware of the Yogurt," *The Economist*, May 19, 2011.

highest state taxes in the country, runs an overburdened and increasingly unworkable pension system for public employees, and maintains regulatory and environmental laws that discourage economic development. Texas has enacted tort reform to reduce the incidence of frivolous lawsuits, has avoided some of the worst real estate excesses by mandating that home mortgages not exceed 80 percent of appraised value, and offers a lighter tax and regulatory burden. During the past two decades its economy has grown at the annual rate of 3.3 percent, compared with America's overall figure of 2.6 percent for the same period.[16]

Another major area for domestic reform concerns energy consumption. Effective measures can be taken to lessen oil imports, decrease carbon emissions, and promote the development of domestic energy resources and employment, but myths abound, for example, concerning the perennially proclaimed goal of energy independence. Here too, political clichés are of little value. Complete energy independence is neither necessary nor possible. Instead, in the context of a worldwide oil market, the most important consideration is to reduce both America's dependence on imported oil and its vulnerability to oil price and supply disruptions. Moreover, the enormous sums spent on importing oil not only burden the balance of payments; they also provide huge revenues that help keep despotic petro-state regimes in power. What is needed is a diverse, robust energy mix that includes better efficiency at home (that is, improved conservation) coupled with increased domestic energy production, especially of oil and natural gas, along with the safe use of nuclear power. Renewable energy resources such as wind and solar power have a useful place in this energy mix, but compared with the vast quantities of energy required to sustain modern American life, none of these provides a magic bullet and their overall impact will remain modest, at least for the medium term. The challenge is to focus on what is practical and effective, rather than on what is fashionable or politically expedient.

---

[16] See Jay Ambrose, "The Texas vs. California Example," *Orange County Register*, and *Scripps Howard News Service*, June 13, 2011, http://www.realclearpolitics.com/articles/2011/06/13/the_texas_example_110182.html, accessed June 15, 2011. Also see "A Texas Roundhouse for the Trial Lawyers," and "The Lone Star Jobs Surge," *The Wall Street Journal*, June 3 and June 6, 2011.

Natural gas offers immense promise and as a result of the recent surge in the exploration and production of deep, or shale, gas reserves, its use for energy generation has been rapidly expanding. Despite environmental concerns, these gas resources can be exploited safely and effectively and can be a welcome source of jobs and economic development.

Nuclear power emits no greenhouse gasses and has a necessary place in providing reliable base-load electrical capacity, although as the 2011 Fukushima nuclear disaster reminds us, nuclear facilities must be operated and managed with rigorous safety standards. Nuclear waste is the industry's Achilles' heel, but permanent storage arrangements for the Yucca Mountain nuclear waste repository have been blocked more by political than technical obstacles, after three decades and $15 billion have been spent on the project.

For direct reduction of both oil imports and consumption, automobile fuel efficiency is critical, since some two-thirds of oil use takes place in the transport sector. Increases in the miles per gallon (mpg) requirement for new cars and light trucks have been important, and the long-term cumulative effect of these measures (as noted in Chapter 2) will be quite substantial. In addition, price signals matter greatly, and increasing the federal gasoline tax at the pump can reinforce the incentives for individuals to choose fuel-efficient vehicles and to be cost-effective in their driving habits. The idea of such a tax increase is, however, intensely unpopular.

Despite practical energy options, examples of ill-advised and counterproductive policies abound. The subsidy for ethanol fuel provides little or no net benefit in energy efficiency, reduction of greenhouse gasses, or lessening dependence on imports of foreign oil. Conversely, by consuming nearly 40 percent of the domestic corn crop, ethanol fuel production has contributed to higher food prices at home and problems for poorer food-importing countries. Solar and wind power have their uses, but much of the emphasis on them is driven by fashion and subsidy rather than efficiency. For purposes of electricity generation, neither is cost-competitive with natural gas, coal, or hydroelectricity. Although the operation of wind and solar power produces no direct greenhouse gases, some does occur in their manufacture. In addition, both have their own drawbacks: Wind turbines require large amounts of steel, take up substantial land or maritime areas, produce noise, and kill large numbers of migratory birds. Solar can be a valuable source for some applications, but for base-load electrical capacity, huge land areas would be required for the arrays of solar collectors, and solar is even less cost-competitive than wind power. In addition, with current technology, solar is not productive at night or at times when the sun is not shining, and transmitting electrical power from these solar and wind sites often entails the building of costly new transmission lines. A less high-tech but often more cost-efficient use of solar power is for hot water heating, although this has received far less promotion and subsidy than photovoltaics.

Ironically, although about 10 percent of America's electricity is provided by renewables, the majority of that comes from hydroelectricity rather than wind or solar. Unfortunately, production of hydropower has declined by approximately one-third since the late 1990s, with the result that the United States now produces less electricity from renewables than it did in 1997.[17] In this case, a greater national good – a clean, reliable base-load supply of nonpolluting, domestically produced, and efficient electricity – has been losing out to a less essential set of preferences (protection for fish and opportunities for recreational waterways).

Immigration reform would be another valuable step on any serious agenda of needed domestic change, and, as with other key policy proposals, it is a subject that triggers sharp partisan disagreements. Historically, immigrants have contributed greatly to American society. They have been a source of entrepreneurship, vibrancy, and cultural enrichment, and their presence has helped keep the United States growing and dynamic. In recent decades, immigrants from China and India have played a major role in the successes of Silicon Valley and more than half the current workforce there is from abroad. In addition, although just 12 percent of the American population is foreign-born, 70 percent of recent finalists in the Intel Corporation's national talent search student competition have been children of immigrants.[18]

---

[17] See Megan McArdle, "The Green Revolution Is Neither," *The Atlantic*, July/August, 2011, p. 48.

[18] The Intel competition replaced an earlier and better-known program run for many years by Westinghouse. See "Brain Gain and Drain," *The Wall Street Journal*, June 3, 2011.

Constructive ideas for dealing with these issues have included expanding the number of H1-B visas for skilled immigrants, offering green-card status to anyone who successfully completes an advanced degree at a U.S. university, and granting residency or citizenship to those who serve honorably in the armed forces. Meanwhile, existing policies remain seriously dysfunctional. They create frustrating bureaucratic obstacles for the skilled and entrepreneurial migrants most valuable to American society, while inadequate border enforcement allows large numbers of poorly educated and illegal immigrants to enter the country.

America needs reforms that will be effective in deterring illegal entrants, provide temporary visas for agricultural and other workers, and favor those best equipped to contribute to and flourish in a modern economy. Eventually, steps will need to be taken to regularize the status of many of the estimated 12 million illegals, who, along with their often U.S.-born children, are unlikely to be successfully deported after long stays in the United States. Such measures are overdue, yet it is by no means clear that they can be managed politically. Liberals are prone to elide the distinction between legal and illegal immigration and to criticize as "anti-immigrant" those measures that seek to address the problem of illegals and borders. Conservatives tend to focus on border security and requirements that employers verify the legal status of immigrant employees. Although they are less inclined to address what is to be done with the large numbers of undocumented immigrants in society, they argue that stricter enforcement would benefit working-class citizens who face job competition from undocumented aliens. They also point to a similar amnesty during the 1980s that had the unintended effect of stimulating still more illegal immigration.

Structural unemployment, particularly for manual workers and those without some college education, poses a serious problem for individuals and the wider society. Much of this is attributable to a long-term trend away from older smokestack industries and toward services and the information economy. The issue is especially acute for unskilled workers and those without even a high school diploma. Despite significant regional differences, reforms in worker training or retraining can be helpful if selectively targeted. Whatever the answers to this stubborn problem, a strong and growing economy is a sine qua non for coping with unemployment. In addition, practical programs to repair and improve infrastructure can boost both employment and economic growth, as can export promotion and expansion of free trade.

Finally, any list of what is to be done at home must include sustaining a culture of innovation and entrepreneurship along with an advanced and resilient scientific and technical base. Continuing support for basic research, science, and medicine, as well as support for major research centers and universities is critical to maintaining America's edge.

What Is to Be Done Abroad

Almost every deliberation about foreign policy sooner or later gives rise to calls for renewed or enhanced reliance on international institutions and multilateralism as the preferred means for addressing common problems and threats. However, while the world may now be more multipolar, it is arguably less multilateral. The number and relevance of actors and chessboards on which world politics, economics, and conflict play out have increased, but there is little sign that the world is becoming better able to manage or mitigate these conflicts. This is evident in the shortcomings of international and regional institutions and the behavior of rising powers. Nonetheless, some liberal internationalist thinkers remain relentlessly optimistic about new forms of collaboration and global governance. As a prime example of this thinking, John Ikenberry of Princeton writes: "More generally, given the emerging problems of the twenty-first century, there will be growing incentives among all the great powers to embrace an open rule-based international system. . . . Growing interdependence in the realm of security is also creating a demand for multilateral rules and institutions."[19] Yet evidence for these emerging forms of cooperation is not easy to discern. The BRICS and others mostly have been conspicuous in their reluctance to cooperate. This was apparent not only in Libya, despite all "necessary action" to protect civilians having been authorized by the UN Security Council, but in other realms as

---

[19] G. John Ikenberry, "The Future of the Liberal World Order: Internationalism after America," *Foreign Affairs* (May/June 2011): 66–67.

well. These include human rights, humanitarian intervention, ethnic cleansing, the environment, enforcement of nuclear nonproliferation agreements, the rule of law, free-trade regimes, and even in China's deliberate undervaluation of the yuan in direct contravention of IMF and WTO rules to which Beijing is supposedly bound.[20]

It thus remains essential to appreciate the uniqueness of America's strengths and status. Even with a degree of erosion in its relative power compared to a generation ago, no other country possesses comparable capabilities. The United States remains the world's principal provider of collective goods, and, contrary to a good deal of wishful thinking, the alternative to American leadership is not that the UN, the EU, the IAEA, or one or more of the rising powers will step forward, but that others cannot or will not do so.

For American foreign policy, this requires both recognition of this reality and a sense of how best to deal with its implications. On the one hand, it is necessary to seek collaboration and burden sharing on important international issues such as nuclear nonproliferation, peacekeeping, failed states, trade and intellectual property rights, and world health, so as not to become overburdened. On the other hand, it remains essential to retain a keen sense of priorities and of the need to be able to act with or without others when effective international cooperation is unattainable.

The evolution of the Obama administration's foreign policy provided evidence of these realities. Barack Obama came to office in January 2009 committed to offering America's adversaries an "extended hand." In doing so, he and his advisors were implicitly relying on what can be termed an interactionist understanding of other countries' foreign policies, assuming that these were largely determined in reaction to what their leaders perceived the United States to be saying and doing rather than as expressions of their own values, history, and interests.[21] The idea seemed to be that if only the new president

---

[20] IMF rules state that, "each member undertakes ... to avoid manipulating exchange rates ... in order to ... gain an unfair competitive advantage over other members." Article IV of *IMF Articles of Agreement*, implemented 1978. Quoted in Roberto Giannetti da Fonseca, "Getting Real," *American Interest* (July/August 2011): 22.

[21] Alexander Dallin and Gail Lapidus defined this type of assumption in "Reagan & the Russians: US Foreign policy Toward the Soviet Union and Eastern Europe,"

could assure adversaries or allies that he – and thus America – means well, threats or problems could be mitigated or overcome altogether. In practice, however, emphasis on interdependence, good intentions, and the belief that "the interests of nations and peoples are shared" did not go very far in explaining the motivations of Vladimir Putin, Mahmoud Ahmadinejad, Bashar al-Assad, or Hugo Chavez.

In a quest to bridge differences, the Obama administration at times slipped into mirror-imaging by underemphasizing the distinction between allies and adversaries, and in seeking to equate very different kinds of responsibility. For example, President Obama's June 2009 Cairo speech suggested Western sources for the region's problems and downplayed local causes such as authoritarianism, corruption, and internal obstacles to social and economic progress. By the end of the following year, the shortcomings of this view would become obvious with the eruption of the Arab Spring.

Initially, the Obama administration had reached out to Iran, Syria, Russia, North Korea, Venezuela, and others, in the expectation that a more positive expression of America's purpose would cause things to change. This orientation, along with an emphasis on international institutions and multilateral cooperation, prioritized processes of liberal internationalism over liberalism's substantive core values including human rights, liberty, democracy, and solidarity with like-minded allies. The deficiencies of this approach soon became glaringly evident in Iran, where the Obama administration chose not to make a major issue of the regime's stealing of the June 2009 presidential elections, despite massive public protests by the Iranian people. A subsequent if somewhat mystifying example was to cling to the hope that President Bashar al-Assad of Syria could be a "reformer" rather than the inheritor and sustainer of the brutal, despotic regime put in place by his late father, Hafez al-Assad. Only after the regime had killed thousands of protesters did the administration finally call for Assad to step down.

Over a period of time, the administration found itself having to adjust as it became clear that leaders of Iran, Syria, North Korea,

in Kenneth A. Oye, Robert J. Lieber, and Donald Rothchild (eds.), *Eagle Defiant: United States Foreign Policy in the 1980s* (Little Brown, 1983), pp. 206–207.

China, and Russia were firmly attached to their own agendas and mostly unresponsive to this outreach. Eventually, there were tangible signs of adaptation, as evident in Obama's Afghanistan "surge" announced in December 2009, his acceptance of a schedule for Iraqi troop withdrawal largely inherited from his predecessor, a cautious embrace of change and democracy in the Arab Spring, the successful operation to kill Osama bin Laden without providing advance notice to Pakistani authorities, and reassurance extended to China's East Asian neighbors.

Why the Declinists Are Wrong Again

International institutions, alliances, and balances of power have important uses, but none are by themselves a sufficient substitute for America's unique role. As a consequence, major retrenchment or outright disengagement by the United States would make the world a far more unstable and dangerous place, and more threatening to America's own national interests. The result would be less of the world order that liberal internationalists seek, as well as greater threats to the national security that realist advocates of withdrawal claim to prioritize. Ironically, this may be better appreciated abroad. In the same Gallup survey that found the United States by far the most popular destination for would-be foreign migrants, respondents in more than one hundred countries expressed much higher approval of U.S. leadership than for six other major powers including (in order), Germany, France, Japan, the United Kingdom, China, and Russia.[22]

The American role remains – in the oft-used word – indispensable. It is important not to devalue or underestimate the importance of the United States in world affairs. With its leadership and hard power

---

[22] Forty-seven percent of respondents expressed approval of the United States, 25% disapproved, and 21% did not know or respond. For China, the figures were 31% approval, 17% disapproval, and 33% did not know or respond. Russia rated even lower at 27%, 31%, and 33% for the respective categories. See Jon Clifton, "Worldwide Approval of U.S. Leadership Tops Major Powers." [NB: Gallup data for 100 countries. Country scores to do not add to 100% because not all respondents named each of the countries surveyed.] See *Gallup.com*, March 24, 2011, http://www.gallup.com/poll/146771/Worldwide-Approval-Leadership-Tops-Major-Powers.aspx, accessed June 21, 2011.

resources, it is the ultimate guarantor against aggressive and nihilistic movements and regimes. This reality was captured by Robert Gates, as he prepared to step down as Secretary of Defense:

> If history and religion teach us anything, it is that there will always be evil in the world, people bent on aggression, oppression, satisfying their greed for wealth and power and territory, or determined to impose an ideology based on the subjugation of others and the denial of liberty to men and women.... But make no mistake, the ultimate guarantee against the success of aggressors, dictators, and terrorists in the 21st century, as in the 20th, is hard power – the size, strength, and global reach of the United States military.[23]

All the same, given the experiences of the post–Cold War and post-9/11 decades, indispensability does not equate with omnipotence or invincibility. Over-commitment poses a risk as well. There exists a cyclical dynamic, in which American dominance tends to be overestimated in the aftermath of prodigious success. The most obvious cases include the initial months after victories in World Wars I and II, the period between the end of the Cuban Missile Crisis in October 1962 and the 1965 escalation in Vietnam, the end of the Cold War in 1989, and following the successive defeats of Saddam Hussein's forces in 1991 and 2003.

The maintenance of domestic support also is critical. No foreign policy can be sustained if it lacks sufficient backing. Maintaining a solid domestic base remains the sine qua non for a leading world role. This includes the interplay of material and ideational elements. The material dimension requires a strong and dynamic economy at home, as well as the requisite technological and military strength. Essential foreign commitments need to be maintained while avoiding overextension. The ideational dimension entails leadership and the appreciation and expression of American interests, security, and national purpose. This includes not only the effective use of traditional diplomacy, but public diplomacy as well. Information-age ideas about the world as a global village (as in the Clinton era) or focus on social media (as during the Obama presidency) are all well and good, but they do not

---

[23] Robert Gates, Commencement Speech, University of Notre Dame, May 22, 2011, http://newsinfo.nd.edu/news/22018-robert-gates-commencement-address/, accessed June 16, 2011.

provide effective substitutes for focused and well-conceived programs to convey American values and purpose.

Despite daunting problems at home and abroad, there remain compelling reasons why the United States is not likely to find itself in an irreversible state of decline. Absent some extraordinary and hitherto unimaginable ("black swan") event, America's history and fundamental strengths are likely to be a more reliable guide to the future than any number of pessimistic assessments. This is not to disparage the more thoughtful expressions of concern that have emerged during the past decade, but even some of the most astute observers have underestimated both the resilience and sense of purpose of the United States. Moreover, public and elite reactions to the 9/11 attacks on New York and Washington, and, nearly a decade later, the expressions of national satisfaction in the killing of Osama bin Laden suggest the reservoirs of national solidarity that exist, whatever the sometimes dysfunctional levels of partisanship and political animosity.

Crisis can also be a stimulus to change, and it is often the case that major problems are not grappled with effectively until they become acute. Coping with debt, deficit, and entitlements could well fit this pattern. These issues are not by themselves insurmountable, despite the political obstacles to resolving them.

In foreign affairs, although the dangers from nuclear proliferation and terrorism are serious, and the rise of regional powers makes it more difficult for the United States to gain agreement on multilateral approaches to common problems, there is no real peer competitor on the horizon, other than China. Despite a challenging array of security threats, America retains military strength and power projection capacities that continue to dwarf those of potential rivals. Therefore, the ultimate determinants of America's staying power are likely to be less those of material resources than of policy and will.

Over the years, America's staying power has been repeatedly underestimated. Pessimistic forecasts in previous eras have been wrong, and it is likely that contemporary declinist assessments will prove to be similarly mistaken. As is dramatically evident in such realms as energy, economics, and security, and potentially in coping with disease, environmental crises, cyber attacks, or the spread of chemical, biological, nuclear, or radiological weapons, events occurring halfway around the globe have the potential to impact quickly and directly on American society. To play an engaged, direct, and forward-leaning international role thus remains of critical importance, and appreciating the capacity of the United States to sustain such a role is essential. Despite real problems, America retains its edge, and its advantages include both material and nonmaterial elements. Much remains to be done in domestic as well as foreign policy, but the robustness of American society coupled with its unique capacities for adaptation and adjustment are likely once again to prove decisive.

Index